For those who preach and  s written an inspiring and re tion of the Word. This boo to preach is to inflect the W just in communication but ... ...Incarnation. Indeed, Koessler challenges us with the inspiring and sobering truth that to preach is to prepare others for eternity.

Dr. Chris Brauns, Pastor, The Red Brick Church,
Stillman Valley, Illinois; author, *Unpacking Forgiveness*
and *When the Word Leads Your Pastoral Search*

Preaching is the sweetest agony in the world. I know of nothing that is more rewarding, more haunting, more ego smashing, and more gratifying than the ministry of proclamation. Every once in a while a book on preaching comes along that helps us ramp up the sweetness and reduce the agony. John Koessler's *Folly, Grace, and Power* is one of those books. Whether you are a seasoned preacher or just getting started, if you care about being an effective preacher, this book is a must-read for you.

Dr. Joseph M. Stowell, President, Cornerstone University

John Koessler reminds us that preaching is nothing less than raising the dead. This book makes me want to preach! *Folly, Grace, and Power* will give you fresh courage to preach your guts out through the power that Jesus supplies.

Justin Buzzard, Lead Pastor, Garden City Church,
San Jose; blogger, *BuzzardBlog*

John Koessler has written a fine book, an unyielding reminder that preachers are theologians who must not capitulate to the idols of popularity or success, and a steady encouragement that God uses the foolishness of preaching to minister with grace and power. This well-written book is thoughtful, full of images, blending narrative and proposition will help pastors meditate on their calling.

Jeffrey Arthurs, Professor of Preaching and Communication,
Chair of the Division of Practical Theology,
Gordon-Conwell Theological Seminary

Once, years ago, I toured a nuclear power plant. I didn't see *power*, of course, but I saw the astonishing interior engineering of power before it courses out to our homes. This book, *Folly, Grace, and Power*, took me into the interior powerhouse of preaching. John Koessler's vivid language and freshly wrapped theology of preaching made me restless for next Sunday and the pulpit that awaits me.

Lee Eclov, Pastor, Village Church of Lincolnshire

Finally! A book for communicators of God's Word that addresses theology more than tactics, the divine more than the delivery.

Dave Johnson, Senior Pastor,
River of Life Church, Elk River, Minnesota

John Koessler is onto something. Most preaching texts focus on homiletical techniques but lack a substantial theology of preaching. Koessler's volume helps us understand why we do what we do when we stand up to preach. I was especially moved by his chapter Speaking for the Silent God. As a whole, this book reinforced my convictions, challenged some of my assumptions, bolstered my confidence, tempered my pride, and filled in gaps in my theology of preaching. It has inspired me to keep preaching the Word and to keep teaching and encouraging a new generation of pastors to do the same.

Steven D. Mathewson, author,
The Art of Preaching Old Testament Narrative

In *Folly, Grace, and Power* John Koessler gives us a theology of preaching that can rescue the voice of the church from the mechanical drone of informative but powerless lectures, and from cliché spiritual soundbites that neither challenge nor transform. The church needs to listen carefully to John's words, which can, by God's grace, restore dignity to the prophetic and priestly work of proclamation by giving us a compelling picture of the nature, value, place, power, and mystery of preaching God's Word.

Joe Thorn, author, *Note to Self: The Discipline of Preaching to Yourself*

Koessler opens up preaching's paradox of folly, grace, and power by stimulating us to think theologically. Several times this book made me pause and wonder. Well-written, wearing its scholarship lightly, it makes a theology of preaching accessible and sparkles with deft quotations and issues that all preachers should wrestle with.

Michael J. Quicke, CW Koller Professor of Preaching,
Northern Seminary

John Koessler's *Folly, Grace, and Power* is filled with realism, truth, and hope. Realism because it does not shun hard topics, such as death, to which it devotes a chapter. It speaks truth to those who preach to a generation who are unsure about truth. And above all, this book is infused with the hope that comes from trusting the Spirit to use the Word to work immeasurably more than all we ask or imagine (Eph. 3:21). And if you ask me whether it is well written, my answer is, It sparkles!

Robert A. Peterson, Professor of Systematic Theology,
Covenant Theological Seminary;
Pastor, Country Bible Church, Bunker Hill, Illinois

FOLLY, GRACE, AND POWER

FOLLY, GRACE, AND POWER

The Mysterious Act of Preaching

JOHN KOESSLER

Foreword by Dr. Bryan Chapell

ZONDERVAN®

ZONDERVAN.com/
AUTHORTRACKER
follow your favorite authors

ZONDERVAN

Folly, Grace, and Power
Copyright © 2011 by John Koessler

This title is also available as a Zondervan ebook. Visit www.zondervan.com/ebooks.

This title is also available in a Zondervan audio edition. Visit www.zondervan.fm.

Requests for information should be addressed to:

Zondervan, *Grand Rapids, Michigan* 49530

Library of Congress Cataloging-in-Publication Data

Koessler, John, 1953–
    Folly, grace, and power : the mysterious act of preaching / John Koessler.
    p. cm.
    Includes bibliographical references (p. 143–150).
    ISBN 978-0-310-32561-1 (softcover) 1. Preaching. I. Title.
BV4211.3.K62 2011
251—dc22 2011010574

Published in association with the literary agency of Mark Sweeney & Associates, Bonita Springs, Florida 34135.

Cover design: *Tammy Johnson*
Cover photography or illustration: *Randy Faris/CORBIS*
Interior design: *Michelle Espinoza*

Printed in the United States of America

11 12 13 14 15 16 17 18 /DCI/ 20 19 18 17 16 15 14 13 12 11 10 9 8 7 6 5 4 3 2 1

For Michael Reed and Kerwin Rodriguez
I am proud to have been your teacher and blessed to be your friend.

CONTENTS

FOREWORD

Every veteran preacher knows the experience: you have just preached the sermon that you are sure will send the elders board scurrying to nominate a pulpit committee to find your replacement. You also wonder how you could have managed to be so dull and so lacking in insight or inspiration. You went through the motions of preaching, but there was no fire in your gut and no joy in your performance. Afterward, you stand at the rear door of the sanctuary thirsty for the regulars to give their clichéd and halfhearted, "Good sermon, pastor." Though the words usually turn your stomach, you know that today these forced courtesies will provide the only drops of hope that there is any reason for you ever to return to the pulpit. But then, extended from the line of limp handshakes, comes a hand that takes yours with an energy that seems determined to reach into your heart. Teary eyes meet yours and a grateful voice says, "Pastor, how did you know just what to say to ease my pain? I had given up hope, but you have given me reason to live again. Thank you for that word from God."

Of course, the opposite can occur. You imagine that the sermon you have just preached will surely qualify for the next anthology of messages meant to identify the modern successors of Whitfield and Spurgeon. But then, while your thumbs grow red from being hooked behind suspenders stretched taut by a chest puffed with pride, the line of parishioners passes in silence. No one mentions the oratorical masterpiece they have just heard, and your ego deflates as rapidly as your estimation of the judgment of your listeners. All you know for certain is that this preaching business is a mystery. Something beyond natural processes governs the way the human heart receives God's Word.

The apostle Paul confirms the mystery when he relates that "natural" humanity—those persons in whom the Spirit of God is not working—hears the truths of the gospel as foolishness and cannot understand its significance. Paul writes, "The natural person does not accept the things of the Spirit of God, for they are folly to him, and he is not able to understand them because they are spiritually discerned" (1 Cor. 2:14 ESV).

Natural reason, natural inclinations, and human nature will reject the gospel unless some force beyond human reason, instinct, and nature gets involved. The message that, despite our sin, we can be reconciled to a holy God by faith in a Savior who rose from the dead two thousand years ago sounds ridiculous to anyone who is not made receptive to this good news by the Holy Spirit.

Not only are the things of God foolishness to humanity apart from the supernatural influence of the Spirit, they cannot be known without the Holy Spirit's provision. This is not a matter of ignorance; a Christian is not smarter than other people. Rather, people are incapable of perceiving as sensible or true what God's Word communicates about Christ's provisions unless the Holy Spirit opens appropriate receptors in heart and mind.

The apostle Paul contends that the spiritual dimensions of truth cannot be recognized for their true significance without an inward change of heart. Until the synapses of the soul have been completed by the inward work of the Spirit, persons have a profound inability to perceive the spiritual realities that are actually present. Comparable to the mysteries of those "magic eye" optical illusions, a reality exists beyond the ordered dots of religious tradition that first strike human perception. With the illusion, one hopes that the synapses of the brain ultimately will connect in such a way that the surface image dissolves away. Then, an entirely different three-dimensional object appears with color and depth that the natural eye previously had no ability to see. Similarly, the internal changes wrought by the Holy Spirit upon the soul enable the individual to perceive the realities of eternity previously unknown.

These spiritual dynamics, while remaining mysteriously beyond human control, help us make sense of puzzling aspects of religious perception. We may question, for instance, how some people (including religious scholars) can know so much about the Bible and yet be so blind to and unaccepting of its truths. They may know volumes about the history and doctrines of the faith and yet see it all as a "social construct" or "human fantasy." How can someone know so much about Scripture and understand so little about the realities of faith? The answer from the apostle is that one can describe with great expertise the surface patterns of the text (similar to describing an optical illusion as having 3549 dots in eight colors on an eight-by-ten expanse) without actually seeing what the text reveals. <u>Until the Spirit of God has turned a heart of stone into a heart of flesh (Ezek. 11:19; 36:26), the person has no ability to see and respond to the spiritual realities in the text.</u> Such people are "always learning but never able to acknowledge the truth" (2 Tim. 3:7).

At a more personal and pastoral level, the knowledge that the Spirit must overcome natural human inability to make spiritual realities anything more than foolishness to ordinary perception may relieve us from the concern that the only reason that loved ones, a church, or a community are not responding to the gospel is that we must be doing something wrong. While it is possible that our message or presentation is flawed, it is also possible to say and do everything right and still face those who do not have eyes to see or ears to hear (Isa. 6:9; Ezek. 12:2; Matt. 13:13).

While these truths may help to make sense of the way some people react to the gospel, it may also demotivate our proclamation of it. We might well reason, "Why should I bother to share the gospel with someone, if I do not know that the Spirit is working in them? My words are just going to bounce off wooden ears if the Spirit has not made them able to hear." One answer to such questioning is the fact that we do not know if the Spirit has made people able to receive his truth, so it behooves us to obey God by proclaiming what he may be enabling them to perceive. The other more motivating response is that the Holy Spirit uses the proclamation of his Word to quicken the human spirit to receive gospel truths.

Through Scripture, the Spirit of God reveals a love that is beyond our conjuring or fathoming. This is wonderful but also a problem. For what good is accomplished by revealing wonders that cannot be received? $E=mc^2$ may be a wonderful revelation, but it is useless if you're telling it to a first-grader whose mind cannot handle such truths. This is why Paul tells us that the truths of Scripture "are *spiritually* discerned" (1 Cor. 2:14, emphasis mine) by virtue of the Holy Spirit's work. By giving us his Spirit for understanding, God makes us able to comprehend his revelation (1 Cor. 2:10 – 12). The Spirit works by and with the Word in our hearts to give us comprehension of the significance of the gospel.

Through Scripture, God supplies a heavenly peg of revelation to go into a human hole of understanding. This will not work, of course, if that's the totality of the process. A heavenly revelation will no more go into human comprehension than a square peg will go into a round hole. So God gives us his Spirit to conform our understanding to the dimensions of his revelation. The same Spirit who inspired the Word opens the heart to receive it and enables the mind to understand it.

While human factors can darken understanding, they do not preclude right comprehension of eternal truths, because the same Spirit who gave the revelation is the one who enables the heart to receive it. The Holy Spirit supernaturally transcends the limitations of the natural order by originally inspiring the Word and subsequently illumining our understanding of it.

When we realize that the supernatural work of the Holy Spirit is the necessary and sufficient provider of spiritual understanding, then we rightly question those who claim that our ministries will be effective so long as we have the right marketing strategy or sermon skills or reasoning ability. The Spirit can use strategies, skills, and abilities (all of which are to be faithfully applied to the work of the gospel), but there will always be a mystery beyond human fathoming of how, when, and why the Spirit works. We may build human empires and manipulate human behavior with human skills, but the Spirit alone can open the heart and mind to spiritual truth, and he blows supernaturally and where he will (John 3:8).

Our spiritual power is not a product of secret formulas discovered at the end of some human quest or through the intricacies of human philosophy. We serve the Spirit's purposes when we "express spiritual truths in spiritual words." The power of supernatural transformation is in the truth of the message itself. I need to remember this when I am tempted to think the reason I will be heard is my cleverness, or when I fail to speak because I believe my thoughts are inadequate. The work of the Spirit occurs as we simply remain faithful to expressing the spiritual truths of Scripture.

In recent years, I have grown more and more to love the power of the simple message of the gospel, to speak to people of heaven and hell, the sin of our hands, the blood of our Savior, and the grace of the God who freely provided mercy so that we might be forgiven. I am steadily more convinced that the truths of Scripture have innate power because they have the blessing of the Spirit, not because of the skill of human delivery. Still, if I am not careful and prayerful, I can fall back into feeling as though I need a better word, a more convincing argument, a more contemporary message, or a more respectable gospel. So those moments when the Spirit blesses hearts despite my sense of failure, or seems silent despite my self-congratulation, are the times to bow before the reminder that what is, and always will be, needed is the power of the Spirit in the Word itself.

Yet even if we believe in the power of the message, we can doubt the adequacy of the messenger. We may run from the task or seek greater effectiveness in purely human techniques not because we believe in any deficiency in the message but because we doubt the adequacy of the human messenger. On such occasions, we must remember the natural instruments as well as the scriptural words that are means of the Spirit's supernatural power.

Our skills or inadequacies ultimately are not the determiners of the power of the preached Word. Paul says God put his message in "jars of clay to show that this all-surpassing power is from God and not from us" (2 Cor. 4:7). I do not understand all of how it happens that God can take words from human lips and make them into instruments of divine transformation that will change the eternal destinies of souls. But that is the way it works, even if I cannot explain how. God may conform our thought to his own, or he may give us words we did not plan to say, or he may channel our choice of words so aptly to coincide with the needs of our listeners that they are astounded by the suitability of our message for their situation. The Spirit may winnow chaff from our words even as they enter another mind so that what actually enters the heart of that person germinates as God's own pure wisdom. By such processes and ten thousand more, the Spirit continues his supernatural superintendence of his Word so that by merely preaching the truth of God's Word, he gives his people precisely what they need to hear.

Our minds object that this aptitude of speech for so many different persons in so many different situations is not humanly possible. We have neither the wisdom nor skill to speak so fitly to so many. We do not know our listeners' situations so intimately, and we do not know God's purposes so thoroughly, that we can speak of what so many hearts need with appropriate care. We remain too weak, ignorant, and sinful to be adequate instruments of God's purposes. Yes, this is all true. Yet despite our weakness, failings, and sin, the Spirit works through and beyond us. That is why the truth of Scripture may succeed when our pulpit delivery limps, and why our oratorical flourishes are not determinative of the Spirit's actual effects.

The truths of Scripture we proclaim accomplish the purposes of the Spirit who gave them. This is the great mystery and blessing of preaching. Its spiritual effects surpass human control, limitation, or explanation. They cannot be bottled, canned, or tamed. And a book that explores this mystery—such a book as this by John Koessler—will bless those who come more fully to appreciate that the unsearchable riches of the Word of God are ours to share through supernatural processes greater than any human scheme, technique, or limitation. Such mystery stimulates our awe, and such awe will generate zeal for this task of eternal consequence.

—Bryan Chapell

PREFACE

The idea for this book grew out of my preparation to teach a course on the theology of preaching. When I turned to my bookshelf for a course text, I found many books on homiletics, but few that looked at preaching through the lens of theology. One of the few was Richard Lischer's *A Theology of Preaching: The Dynamics of the Gospel*, which impressed me with its observation that preaching "suffers a certain theological homelessness."[1] For Lischer, this homeless state is reflected in the myriad subjects linked with homiletics in course catalogs. "It is forever, as one seminary catalogue enumerates with painful clarity, 'Preaching *and*' liturgy, literature, liberation, dance...."[2]

Lischer's description helped me to diagnose something that had been bothering me about the way my students approached preaching. They did not approach preaching as a theological exercise. Instead, they seemed to regard the sermon as if it were little more than a speech about the Bible. As I scanned the tables of contents in the homiletics texts on my shelf and reviewed my own course syllabus, it was easy to see why. Far more attention was devoted to the rhetorical aspects of preaching than to its theological implications. My students had learned homiletical techniques but had no theology of preaching.

I was also impressed by Stephen Webb's *The Divine Voice* and his acknowledgment of the link between the Christian faith and public speaking. As Webb puts it, "Christianity and the fate of public speaking appear to be inextricably linked."[3] Christianity is an oral faith. The gospel, though committed to writing in the Scriptures, is conveyed primarily through proclamation. A decline in Christianity must necessarily lead to a decline in the importance of public speaking. But the reverse must also be true. A decline in the importance of public speaking threatens the future of the Christian faith. Perhaps my students were right after all. Preaching is an exercise in theological rhetoric.

There is a rhetorical dimension to preaching. But there is a divine dimension as well. The words of the preacher remain his own. They are ordinary, human words which retain their fallible quality. Yet they are invested with supernatural power. The preacher's words are not like the words of Scripture. The preacher can err and may obstruct the message. Yet the preacher is convinced that God will speak through the sermon. What is more, and perhaps most mysterious of all, the task of preaching assumes that the preacher is necessary to the task. The preacher provides a living voice for the living Word. When we preach, we inflect the Word of God for those who hear.

The sharp contrast between the common humanity of our words and the unimaginable power of our message is aptly conveyed by Paul when he describes the proclaimed gospel as a treasure in an earthen vessel (2 Cor. 4:7). Our preaching has the capacity to mediate the true presence of Christ. We display "the light of the knowledge of the glory of God in the face of Christ" (2 Cor. 4:6). This dignifies preaching. But it does not elevate the preacher beyond measure. The all-surpassing power comes from God, not from us. We are nothing; God is everything (cf. 1 Cor. 3:7).

This book is an exercise in theological reflection, not an exhaustive treatment. There is much more that could and should be said. If it prompts the preacher and the listener to attend to the sermon with a greater sense of wonder or expectation, it will have accomplished its goal.

chapter 1

FOLLY, GRACE, AND POWER

Tyler died on a Sunday morning. I had just walked in the door when someone called to say there had been an automobile accident and that I should come to the hospital right away. Details were sketchy, but the caller thought it was bad. During the twenty-minute drive to the hospital, I tried in vain to recall Tyler's face. I knew he was one of the children who participated in vacation Bible school, but I didn't think we had ever talked. His mother, Gail, attended our church on and off. His dad, Mike, did not come at all.

I got to the emergency room just as they wheeled the gurney bearing Tyler's lifeless body through the door. Gail gave me a pleading look and a hug. Mike and I shook hands awkwardly as I searched for something comforting to say. What do you say to a mother who has just watched her seven-year-old child die in her arms? How do you explain such a tragedy to a father who on his best day is suspicious of God? How do you tell them that God has not forsaken them? That he is working out some mysterious purpose in their suffering? The only phrases that came to mind seemed trite. So I mumbled a few words of condolence and spent most of the time sitting with the couple in silence, watching them weep and listening as they voiced questions for which I had no answer.

When the time came to preach Tyler's funeral, I stepped to the podium, cleared my throat, and preached the way my homiletics professor taught me in seminary. I did my best to hold out the hope of heaven as the large crowd, most of whom did not attend our church, sat stiff-backed in folding chairs and listened politely. The atmosphere was thick with grief. As I told them about Christ and the cross, my words were interrupted by sobbing. The audience groaned and shrieked, their scattered cries punctuating the gospel like exclamation points. It made me think of accounts I had read of the preaching of Jonathan Edwards. Only in this instance, they were cries of despair, not conviction.

Anyone who has served as a shepherd of God's flock will understand the ambivalence I felt. I was, after all, only a preacher. And what does a preacher have to offer in the face of death besides words? Under the dull-eyed stare of death, all words seem inadequate.

What Is the Matter with Preaching?

Why does it feel as if our preaching seems to accomplish so little, no more potent than a puff of air? Harry Emerson Fosdick, a theological liberal who served as pastor of the historic Riverside Church in New York City, asked this question of the pulpit in his day in a landmark article written for *Harper's Magazine* in 1926 titled "What Is the Matter with Preaching?" The article was notable not only for its content but because of its intended audience. *Harper's* was not a theological or professional journal but a popular magazine. Instead of writing for the pulpit, Fosdick addressed himself to the pew, explaining that listeners far outnumber preachers in the church. "Whatever, therefore, is the matter with preaching is quantitatively far more a concern of laymen than of clergymen," he wrote. "Moreover, if laymen had a clear idea as to the reasons for the futility, dullness, and general ineptitude of so much preaching, they might do something about it. Customers usually have something to say about the quality of goods supplied to them."[1]

Fosdick believed that the sermon should *do* something. He was convinced that every sermon ought to have as its main goal the solving of some human problem. Fosdick, however, did not think that the way to do this was to place the primary focus on the biblical text. Instead, he argued that the preacher should focus on the problem of the audience. "No matter what one's theory about the Bible is," he explained, "this is the searchlight, not so much intended to be looked at as to be thrown upon a shadowed spot."[2]

This metaphor is compelling enough to make expositors blink twice. Have we been so blinded by the searchlight of God's Word, intent as we are upon the text, that we have failed to turn it in the direction of the shadows in our listeners' lives? This might have been true a generation or two ago, but it certainly is not the case with most expositors today. Despite Fosdick's low view of expository preaching, his "project method" is the norm for most modern expositors. Whether we start with the audience or the text, most expositors recognize the importance of identifying congregational needs and addressing them in the sermon. Relevance is not the issue. If anything, we have overcorrected in this area.

Objectifying God

Eugene Peterson makes this argument when he suggests that our real problem is a matter of deafness rather than blindness. God's Word is opened. The sermon is preached. But somehow the voice of God is not heard. Peterson argues that the triune voice of Scripture has been drowned out by a chorus of other voices, a different trinity that is of our own making. "The new Trinity doesn't get rid of God or the Bible," Peterson explains, "it merely puts them to the service of needs, wants, and feelings."[3] Instead of listening for God's voice, we seek to bend the Scriptures to our own will. Peterson warns, "It is entirely possible to come to the Bible in total sincerity, responding to the intellectual challenge it gives, or for the moral guidance it offers, or for the spiritual uplift it provides, and not in any way have to deal with a personally revealing God who has personal designs on you."[4]

Pornography is analogous to the depersonalization and objectification that Peterson is describing. Pornography is the product of the worst kind of utilitarianism. The pornographer's subjects are not really subjects at all but objects. When someone indulges in pornography, he relates to the one in the photograph not as a person but as a thing. Any "relationship" with the image is purely functional—with the gratification of one's own desires as its sole purpose. The human being behind the image remains unseen as far as their relationship to God and to others goes.

Pornography further depersonalizes its subjects by presenting a false face to the world. What is seen is not the true person who posed for the photograph but an airbrushed and unrealistic version of them. Advertising does the same thing by presenting us with images of the body and of life that are beyond unrealistic. In most cases, the body shapes displayed in advertisements are impossible to attain, even for the models who appear in such ads. The photographs have been doctored, as have many of the models themselves, evidenced by supermodel Cindy Crawford's famous remark that she wished she looked like Cindy Crawford when she got up in the morning.

Advertisers practice a kind of reverse objectification by offering the false promise of a relationship with the products they sell. "Ads have long promised us a better relationship via a product: *buy this and you will be loved,*" Jean Kilbourne observes. "But more recently they have gone beyond that proposition to promise us a relationship with the product itself: *buy this and it will love you.*"[5] The problem with this, according to Kilbourne, is that it exploits human desires and needs while promoting a bankrupt concept of relationship.

Preaching does something similar when it hawks God as a product and presents listeners with an "airbrushed" version of the Christian life. This kind of preaching is exemplified in the comment made by one of my son's friends after attending a nearby megachurch. When asked how he liked the service, he complained, "They're just a little too happy there." I knew exactly what he meant. The music is always perky. The sermons are always upbeat. Every serious problem raised during the message is neatly resolved within a matter of minutes, much like the television dramas and commercials that provide the pastor with his themes. This airbrushed portrayal of Christianity is not preaching at all but a form of sentimentalism that trivializes the sermon.

The Trivial Sermon

Jeremy S. Begbie identifies three primary characteristics of what he calls "the pathology of sentimentality." Sentimentalism is marked by a lack of realism, emotionalism, and an avoidance of costly action.[6] Sentimentalism does not ignore the presence of evil, but it cannot bear to look at it in the full light of day. Instead, the sharp contours of tragedy are softened by viewing them in the rosy glow of romanticism or through the sepia-hued filter of nostalgia. Preachers do this when they paint a portrait of Christian experience with the brush of denial, neatly rearranging the shadows in a way that obscures the pain and questioning that often accompany it. Trivialized sermons smooth out the rough edges of the Christian life and offer pat answers to the audience's problems.

Fosdick's approach seems particularly vulnerable to this, assuming as it does that the chief purpose of every sermon is to solve the audience's problems. God is interested in our problems, but preaching does not always solve them. Indeed, it is entirely possible that some preaching, if it is true to Scripture, may actually create problems. When Jesus sent the Twelve out to proclaim the gospel of the kingdom, he gave this warning: "Do not suppose that I have come to bring peace to the earth. I did not come to bring peace, but a sword. For I have come to turn 'a man against his father, a daughter against her mother, a daughter-in-law against her mother-in-law—a man's enemies will be the members of his own household'" (Matt. 10:34–36).

Trivialized preaching is triumphalistic. Triumphalism is a perspective that grows out of our evangelical heritage of revivalism. The revival tradition of preaching emphasizes the transforming moment, when the listener's life is forever changed through an encounter with God through his Word. Certainly this is true of the gospel. We are forgiven in a moment. But the redemptive process takes much longer. Triumphalistic sermons give the impression that any problem can be solved simply by leaving it at the altar. Undoubtedly there have been remarkable instances when this has been the case. Sinners plagued by long-standing habits leave the church miraculously freed from bondage. Yet for many others—perhaps even most others—the experience is different. For them, transformation is progressive rather than instantaneous. These believers do not skip along the pilgrim path but "toil along the winding way, with painful steps and slow."

Preachers who do not acknowledge this resort instead to clichés and platitudes. Their sermon themes are flaccid and the remedies they offer mere placebos. Such sermons are unable to provide any real help to those who hear. How can they, when truism stands in the place of truth? "We live between Eden and heaven, the God who was and the God who will be," Don Hudson reminds us. "In the story that God is telling in our lives, he asks us to live in the stark reality of the cross while we sight the glimmer of the resurrection."[7] To be true to our audience's experience, preaching must reflect the reality of living in a post-Edenic world in anticipation of a new heavens and earth that have not yet come to pass. Our sermons need to explore the full scope of the redemptive experience, encompassing not only the triumph of resurrection Sunday but the brutal pain of Good Friday and the divine silence of Holy Saturday.

Preaching in the Light of Suffering

This may sound strange to us. Protestants have long criticized Roman Catholics for "keeping Christ on the cross" in their theology of the sacraments. Shouldn't evangelical preaching be marked by an emphasis on Christ's victory over the grave? The answer is yes and no. Certainly Christ's resurrection is the heart of Christian preaching. More will be said about this later when we consider the relationship between preaching and the gospel. Nevertheless, suffering is also an integral aspect of the church's experience.

One reason suffering cannot be avoided in the Christian life is because we live in a world that has been broken by sin. Christ's offering of himself on the cross is the true and only remedy for this problem, one that will eventually eradicate sin from our experience. But for now we must live "in-between" in a world that longs for a transformation that is yet to take place (Rom. 8:22–23). Christ's shed blood cleanses us from every sin, but it does not immunize us from the ravages of sin. The same Bible that declares Christ's victory over the grave describes a world in which those who follow Christ also struggle with their sins and suffer the consequences of the sins of others. Paul rebukes Peter for his hypocrisy, and James condemns rich Christians for treating the poor with contempt in the assembly (Gal. 2:11–14; James 2:1–4). Members of the remarkably gifted Corinthian church fight with one another over their favorite preachers and live morally inconsistent lives (1 Cor. 3:1–4; 5:1). All of this takes place *after* Christ's resurrection.

Indeed, Christ's victory over the grave guarantees a measure of suffering for those who follow him. Devotion to Christ may lead to persecution and death (Acts 12:1–2; Rev. 6:10–11). Far from expecting Christ's victory to exempt him from suffering, Paul saw what he experienced for the sake of the gospel as an extension of Christ's suffering (2 Cor. 1:5; Col. 1:24). Suffering is part of the chain of grace that Paul describes in Romans 5:1–5.

Preaching which calls for no sacrifice and prepares for no suffering is both dishonest and dangerous. Preachers whose chief aim is to offer neat solutions to their audiences' problems risk replacing truth with caricature. Instead of preparing God's people to live out their redemption in the real world, they offer a theme-park vision of what it means to follow Jesus. This view does not resemble the true Christian life, any more than Disney World's Main Street resembles life in America today (or at any time). Such preaching may offer a kind of cheap comfort to those who hear it but ultimately provides no real help. It will not prepare a young mother to face the death of her seven-year-old son. Nor will it prepare her to face her own death.

Preaching as Call and Response

Preaching that celebrates the victory of Easter Sunday without forgetting the pain of Good Friday and the silence of Holy Saturday is preaching that refuses to ignore Christ's terrible cry of dereliction from the cross (Matt. 27:46; Mark 15:34). Helmut Thielicke describes these words of Jesus as "more of a shriek than a saying."[8] On the surface, Christ's words sound as if they are in sharp contrast to those he uttered just a few hours earlier when he took bread and gave thanks before breaking it and distributing it to his disciples (Matt. 26:26). Jesus also took the cup, gave thanks and offered it to the disciples, saying, "Drink from it, all of you. This is my blood of the covenant, which is poured out for many for the forgiveness of sins" (Matt. 26:27–28). Do we really believe that the Savior did this blindly, without having in view the bodily suffering he was about to undergo?

Jesus gave thanks for the bread that represented his body, which would be pummeled and torn for the sake of others. He gave thanks for the cup that represented the blood he was about to spill. This heavy cup of sorrow and distress would eventually make his knees buckle and drive him facedown on the ground (Matt. 26:39). Jesus gave thanks for the *cup*.

In Christ's passion, we see sincere gratitude mixed with the sober anticipation of suffering. The Son of God didn't divorce these realities of joy and suffering, and neither should we as the children of God today. If our sermons are to genuinely reflect the experience of those who have received the grace of Christ, they too must carry both lines. Our sermons must proclaim the hope of the gospel even as they give voice to the hard questions our listeners are afraid to speak aloud. The preacher may stand alone behind the pulpit, but with him are all the weighty and tragic realities of the lives of the worshipers in the pews. Preaching may sound like a monologue, but it is really a dialogue between the preacher and the listener.

But there is a third and even more important voice that must be evident in the sermon. There is the voice of God, who speaks through his Word and by his Spirit. Karl Barth underscores this when he defines the sermon as "God's own speaking."[9] For Barth, preaching is a divine event. He acknowledges that there is a human element to the process. The words used in the sermon are the preacher's own words, and those who hear come with their own concerns and must feel that they have been addressed in a vital way. "All these things may well happen in a sermon, of course," Barth warns, "but they are acts which God himself wills to perform and which can never, therefore, be a human task."[10]

We worry that Barth has overstated his case. Surely there is something we can do to confront our listeners with the reality of God. The strength of our conviction on this matter is easily confirmed by scanning the table of contents of any contemporary homiletics text. As helpful as such texts are, it is hard not to come away from them without the impression that preaching is simply an exercise in exegesis and rhetoric.

The truth is, those who preach are in an awkward position, caught between two independent forces and unable to control either of them. On the one side is God, on whose behalf the preacher speaks. On the other is the congregation, which expects God to speak through the preacher. We who preach have the freedom to craft our sermons, but we do not control the message. We may use our own language and select illustrations. We can draw whatever applications seem suitable to us. But we cannot say whatever we please. This is what Calvin means when he says that those who declare God's Word "are not to bring anything of themselves, but to speak from the Lord's mouth."[11]

Even we do not always like what we have to say. Like the prophet Balaam, we are bound by office to the Word of God (Num. 22:38). And like him, we sometimes find ourselves wanting to say one thing, yet being compelled to say the opposite. How many times have we wrestled with God's Word like Jacob wrestling with the angel, refusing to let go until he has blessed us, only to be left scratching our heads wondering why God chose to say *that*. We are confounded by God's choice of words almost as often as we are at a loss for our own.

Folly, Grace, and Power

The climate of worship in which we are called to deliver our message does not help matters. The preacher seems increasingly out of place in the contemporary church, as superfluous to the church's worship as the cadre of seventeen preachers Huck Finn imagined served the king of England. When Mary Jane Wilks marveled at such a large number and the time it would take them to complete the service, Huck told her that not all of them preached.

"Well, then, what does the rest of 'em do?"

"Oh, nothing much. Loll around, pass the plate—and one thing or another. But mainly they don't do nothing."

"Well, then, what are they *for*?"

"Why they're for *style*. Don't you know nothing?"

Is Huck right? Is the preacher there mainly to give the service a sense of style? In some churches today, the sermon feels more like a rhetorical flourish than the culmination of the worship event. The sermon functions as little more than a verbal accent wall in the overall scheme of things. In these settings, it is the worship team, not the preacher, that bears the primary responsibility for mediating God's presence to the congregation. Preaching still has a place. The sermon is a helpful and practical coda to the service. But it is far from being the nucleus of the worship experience. Indeed, there are many in the church who would hardly be disappointed if the entire service were given over to music and the sermon were omitted altogether.

Perhaps we should not be surprised. Despite our careful effort to understand our hearers' problems and to say the right thing in the right way, we have no way of knowing how our words will be received. Will listeners be like the Thessalonians and accept what we say as an oracle of God? Or will they be like the Epicurean and Stoic philosophers who disputed with Paul and asked, "What is this babbler trying to say?" Audiences are fickle. Frame your argument to answer the objections of human reason and they demand a sign. Point to the attesting miracles recorded in Scripture and they argue that such claims are irrational. Paul complained, "Jews demand miraculous signs and Greeks look for wisdom" (1 Cor. 1:22). No wonder Paul characterized preaching as "folly" in light of such conflicting demands.

Still, things are not what they seem. These words which fall upon the ear with a force roughly equivalent to the beat of a hummingbird's wings also have power. God's word spoke worlds into being and raised the dead. Our words likewise exert an influence over the "real" world and have the potential to radically reshape it. Human words have potential to do good and evil. The same lips that can speak "intelligible words to instruct others" and can "confess that Jesus Christ is Lord" are also capable of great corruption (1 Cor. 14:19; Phil. 2:11; James 3:6). Human words are powerful because language has its origin in God. Stephen Webb observes, "Christians believe that all sound has its origin in God because God spoke the world into being."[12] This fact binds the Christian faith to the act of speaking, and in particular to the act of public speaking. According to Webb, "The biblical faith of Christianity is dependent upon our ability to hear the divine voice in the human voice of the preacher. Christianity and the fate of public speaking appear to be inextricably linked."[13] Paul understood the importance of public speaking to the Christian faith but knew that a razor's edge must be walked to keep preaching from devolving into an exercise in rhetoric. "My message and my preaching were not with wise and persuasive words, but with a demonstration of the Spirit's power," he explained, "so that your faith might not rest on men's wisdom, but on God's power" (1 Cor. 2:4–5). Like him, we are dependent upon the Spirit's power not merely for the message but also for the preaching of that message.

Martyn Lloyd-Jones describes the time a Philadelphia printer came to George Whitefield and asked for permission to publish his sermons. Whitefield replied, "Well, I have no inherent objection, if you like, but you will never be able to put on the printed page the lightning and the thunder."[14] This, ultimately, is the basis for our confidence whenever we stand before God's people. Preaching is folly, but it is an intentional folly. Preaching is folly, but it is a folly that saves. We continue to preach because God has bound himself to the preached message and has promised to use it as an instrument of grace and power. The God who spoke the world into being uses our words to bend the world to his will. This is our conviction, despite the fear and trembling we feel when we stand before God's people to declare his Word. Our aim is not merely to instruct, much less to entertain. We are waiting on the lightning and thunder. Our aim is to raise the dead.

chapter 2

THE UNTAMED SPIRIT
AND THE SERMON

Writing the sermon is like the first day of creation. We brood over the message like the Spirit hovering over the waters, dwelling on our words in an effort to wrest life out of chaos and void. What preacher has not felt a stab of panic at the thought of beginning again? It makes little difference that the sermon went well the Sunday before. A successful sermon may actually make us more apprehensive. How do we top that? we wonder. Can the experience be repeated? What should we say next Sunday? What *will* we say? Even worse, once we have said it, how can we be certain that it will be attended by power from on high?

Martyn Lloyd-Jones considered this uncertainty a good thing, a valuable reminder of God's sovereignty in preaching: "You may enter the pulpit feeling really well, confident in your preparation and anticipating a good service, only to have a bad service. There is something wonderful even in that because it shows at any rate that you are not the sole person in control."[1]

The Illusion of Control

There is much in the work of preaching which can lead us to think that we are in control. We analyze texts, choose illustrations, and draw applications. We labor over the structure of the sermon with care, laying the foundation word by word and then building upon it. A few of us even go so far as to choreograph our movements and chart the melody line of our delivery. All of this is in an effort to enhance the "effectiveness" of the message.

The most important aspects of the sermon are out of our hands. We can shape the content of the message, but not how our listeners respond. We have influence over the dynamics of delivery, but not the ebb and flow of the Holy Spirit. He breathes on whomever he wills, and there are many times when we are unable to sense his presence or easily discern his purpose. The audience too is unpredictable in their reaction. One person whose circumstance should make them sympathetic to the ideas expressed in the sermon appears unmoved, while another whom we did not expect to be interested is deeply affected. A sermon which thunders in one service falls flat in another, and we cannot tell why.

We are puzzled by the comments of listeners who express their appreciation for the sermon and try to tell us what God "said" to them during the service. It can be frustrating, after we have wrestled with the history and theology of a text and then worked hard to carefully correlate its implications to the lives of people in our audience, to hear the inferences they themselves draw and realize how removed their conclusions are from our good work. We sometimes wonder if they were listening to us at all. We are tempted to accuse them of confusing our words with those of another, perhaps a sermon they heard on the radio or something they read in a book.

And in fact this may not be far from the truth. The listener's experience with the sermon is not always linear. From our perspective, the sermon is a progression of ideas that moves from beginning to end. We know the whole of what we want to say. No doubt there are many who can follow our train of thought. But for some, our words are more like a bugle call which God uses to awaken ideas he has implanted earlier. Perhaps these ideas were barely noticed at the time. Momentarily lost amid the clamor of daily life, our words have called them forth like Lazarus from the grave. Or maybe they were noted and then carefully filed away for later use until something in the sermon, perhaps even a side remark or an offhand illustration, brings them to mind again. It is as if the Holy Spirit has drawn the listener aside and entered into a private conversation.

Looking for Leverage

In some measure, the entire history of the church's approach to preaching can be explained by a tension between two poles. At one end are those who place the weight of emphasis on human responsibility. They share the conviction of nineteenth-century evangelist Charles Finney, who did not believe that a revival of religion was a miracle but attributed it to the right use of appropriate means.[2] Although he believed it was a mistake to approach revival as if religious feeling could be produced by direct effort, Finney was convinced it could be produced indirectly by training one's attention on the right object. In his *Lectures on Revivals of Religion*, Finney urged readers to rely on a commonsense approach: "It is just as easy to make your minds feel on religion as it is on any other subject. God has put these states of mind just as absolutely under your control, as the motions of your limbs."[3] Consequently, according to Finney, those who listen to the preacher have a responsibility to "break up the fallow ground" of their own hearts before the seed of the Word is sown. If they do not, the preacher is wasting his time: "The farmer might just as well sow his grain on the rock."[4]

Those at the other end of the spectrum emphasize the sovereignty of God in preaching. William Willimon takes issue with Finney and counters, "I am here arguing that revivals *are* miraculous, that the gospel is so odd, so against the grain of our natural inclination and the infatuations of our culture, that nothing less than a miracle is required in order for there to be true hearing."[5] Willimon believes that today's preacher needs to have a "reckless confidence" in the power of the gospel: "We must learn to preach again in such a way as to demonstrate that, if there is no Holy Spirit, if Jesus had not been raised from the dead, then our preaching is doomed to fall on deaf ears."[6]

The theological distance between Finney and Willimon bears witness to the preacher's unenviable position. Though we are required to employ the human tools of reason, argument, and rhetorical skill in the sermon, its outcome rests upon the movement of the untamed Spirit. We are caught between the intransigence of the human heart and the unpredictability of God's Spirit. No wonder some have looked for a way to leverage their words. Finney applied the predictability and methodology of naturalism to spiritual experience in an attempt to discern spiritual mechanics that would ensure results. Like other social reformers of his day, he believed that emotions were the engine of character and could be "shaped through intermediate means."[7]

The cultural landscape has changed even more since Finney's day. Rocked by the tremors of postmodernism, we now live in a world where beliefs and practices are continuously questioned. When the voice of God thundered from Sinai, Moses trembled and all Israel with him. But today's hearer, who recognizes no authority beside his own, dismisses the sound with a shrug and wonders, "Who can say if it is true?" Anthony Giddens observes, "No knowledge under conditions of modernity is knowledge in the 'old' sense, where 'to know' is to be certain."[8] Modern man no longer enjoys the comfort of certitude.

The church has not been immune from this loss of certainty. As a result, there are many today who encourage contemporary preachers to dial down the dogma and rely on induction rather than deduction. Proponents of this "new homiletic" favor story over proposition and dialogue over monologue. They prefer to make their case by appealing to analogies drawn from the hearer's experience. On the surface, this may seem like the antithesis to Charles Finney's lawyerlike argumentation. Yet both approaches depend upon the preacher's skill as a communicator and the listener's ability to grasp what has been said.

The Location of the Spirit's Work

God's Word, of course, includes both proposition and story, employing argument to address reason and narrative to affect the heart. Both exert an important influence on the will. But it is the Spirit, ultimately, who convicts (John 16:8 – 11). Where should we locate the working of the Holy Spirit when it comes to preaching? Does he work primarily on the preacher or on the listener? Is his influence internal or external? Is reason the main sphere of his activity, or does he stir emotion as well? Or is it a combination of all of these?

The apostle Paul identified the preacher as one focus of the Spirit's power when he asked the Ephesians to pray that God would grant him words and boldness in proclamation of the gospel (Eph. 6:19). More is in view with this request than the efficient use of one's natural ability. Paul asks that words or utterance be "given" to him. While such language does not preclude a natural element, it certainly implies more. This is a prayer that God will supply something which would otherwise be absent from Paul's preaching. He expected the Holy Spirit to influence both the content of his message and the manner in which it was delivered.

The Spirit who imparts ability and skill for preaching works in the mind of the preacher to give insight on God's Word. The Bible describes this as knowledge that comes from God and as God-given understanding (1 John 2:20; 1 Cor. 2:14). Theologians use the term *illumination* to distinguish this ministry of the Holy Spirit from his initial work of inspiration. As Grant Osborne explains, "The 'illumination' of the interpreter is one aspect of the larger ministry of the Holy Spirit in bringing people to regeneration and daily growth in their Christian life. It is that portion of the 'internal testimony' which relates to understanding and applying God's revealed Word."[9]

This illumination is not immediate. That is to say, it does not normally come without some effort. The preacher must do the work of exegesis and interpretation and may use tools. Even then there is no guarantee that after this prayerful work those "things that are hard to understand" will not remain hard to understand (2 Peter 3:16). God's help is needed (2 Tim. 2:7). Unlike the infallible result of inspiration, there is a possibility that the preacher may err in the conclusions that are drawn. Consequently, the preacher's authority is entirely dependent upon the sermon's agreement with the truth of Scripture. The fact that the Spirit helps us to understand the text does not relieve the congregation of the responsibility to assess our understanding in light of God's Word. If the words of the church's prophets had to be weighed by those who heard, should the words of her preachers be exempt (1 Cor. 14:29)?

The Spirit also helps us to know what bearing the text has upon the audience and how we should address our listeners. Charles Spurgeon used priestly imagery to describe this aspect of the Spirit's work of illumination when he says, "The Spirit of God will teach you the use of the sacrificial knife to divide the offerings; and he will show you how to use the balances of the sanctuary so as to weigh out and mix the precious spices in their proper quantities."[10] This aspect of the Holy Spirit's ministry of illumination enables us to combine the priestly nature of preaching with prophetic responsibility.

The priestly nature of preaching requires a sensitivity to the spiritual condition of our listeners. "You can cast a man down with the very truth which was intended to build him up," Spurgeon warns. "You can sicken a man with the honey with which you meant to sweeten his mouth."[11] At the same time, the preacher's prophetic obligation means that we will not shy away from saying the hard thing when necessary. God's Word is a lamp, but it is also a sword (Ps. 119:105; Heb. 4:12). It strikes as often as it enlightens. Indeed, the one is often the best means of accomplishing the other. The sermon, likewise, wounds as well as heals and must often do the former before it can accomplish the latter.

Experience also shows that the Holy Spirit does not confine his influence to the preacher's study. There are times when the Spirit gives insight in the moment of preaching that changes the direction of the sermon. Like Paul, who "saw" the faith of the lame man in Lystra as he preached and then healed him, we too may discern something in the audience's response or experience a kind of leading during the message that alters the sermon in unexpected ways (Acts 14:9). Or like Jude in the writing of his epistle, we may chart the course which we think the sermon will take while we are still in the study and then feel impelled to change direction once the actual preaching has begun (Jude 1:3).

The Spirit and the Listener

The audience is the other locus of the Spirit's work in preaching. The Spirit who gives insight to the preacher as the sermon is formed exercises a corresponding ministry in the minds and hearts of those who hear as the sermon is being delivered. The Spirit does more than give the listener a cognitive grasp of the ideas in the biblical text. His work of illumination includes the God-given conviction of faith. The same God who opens the door of opportunity is also able to open the heart (Col. 4:3; Acts 14:27; 16:14; 1 Cor. 16:9; 2 Cor. 2:12). He works in the preacher to "give" words and boldness and then through what is preached to produce faith in those who hear. This is what Paul means when he says that his speech and his preaching were marked by a "demonstration of the Spirit's power" (1 Cor. 2:4). This verse contrasts a message whose result can be explained only by the power of the Spirit with one which relies on human persuasion alone.

The preacher appeals to reason and employs persuasive skill when delivering the message, but conviction and conversion ultimately are God's work (Acts 15:3–4; 21:19). The preacher gives voice to the message but is not the source of its power. According to Calvin, the power of the sermon is rooted in the self-authenticating nature of Scripture: "Therefore, illumined by his power, we believe neither by our own nor by any one else's judgment that Scripture is from God; but above human judgment we affirm with utter certainty (just as if we were gazing upon the majesty of God himself) that it has flowed to us from the very mouth of God by the ministry of men."[12]

Does this mean that God bypasses reason (what Calvin calls "judgment") to produce faith? Reason is not the cause of faith, but it does not follow from this that faith is experienced apart from reason. Our message does not consist of men's wisdom, but it is a message of wisdom (1 Cor. 2:4–7). The distinction Paul makes in 1 Corinthians 14:14–15 in connection with the practice of speaking in tongues reveals the importance of the mind in spiritual experience. The mind and the spirit are not identical. Where the practice of tongues was concerned, it was possible for spiritual activity to occur which the mind did not understand (1 Cor. 14:2). Neither is what Paul refers to as the "mind" in these verses identical with the functions of the brain. Since this activity of the spirit was expressed as speech, presumably the brain was involved. Yet Paul says that in this exercise of uninterpreted tongues, the spirit prayed, but not the mind. As a result, the mind was "unfruitful" (1 Cor. 14:14). What Paul calls the mind is equivalent to understanding. Understanding is required to give assent ("say 'Amen'") to what has been expressed (1 Cor. 14:16).

What was true of tongues is also true of preaching. The mind must be addressed as well as the spirit if those who hear are to benefit from what has been said. The sermon addresses the mind because it aims for understanding. But the mind is not its only target. God's Spirit also uses the sermon to stir the heart. The Word of God gains entry by the gate of the mind, but its ultimate target is the heart, where faith is exercised (Rom. 10:10). We understand with the mind, but we believe with the heart. This is the domain of "holy affections," characterized by Jonathan Edwards as that faculty of the soul "by which it views things, not as an indifferent unaffected spectator, but either as liking, or disliking; approving, or disapproving."[13] Because the mind and the heart together are the sphere in which true faith is experienced, the sermon must address both. It was when those who heard Peter's sermon on the day of Pentecost were "cut to the heart" that they asked, "Brothers, what shall we do?" (Acts 2:37).

Reading Peter's sermon, however, one cannot help noticing that there is little in it which seems emotionally compelling by modern standards. It is remarkably short.[14] Its structure is simple, consisting primarily of a summary of the bare details of Jesus' ministry, supported by Scripture quotations. There are no illustrations or stories other than Jesus' own story, which is recounted factually with few descriptive details. It is certainly not a narrative in the sense that we usually think of one today. It is possible, of course, that Peter assumed that such details were unnecessary and that Jesus' life and ministry were already well known to his listeners. These things had not been "done in a corner" (Acts 26:26).

Yet there is clearly an emotional edge to Peter's message. His declaration that the events his listeners had just witnessed were described in Joel's prophecy must have had a powerful effect on those who waited with expectation for the fulfillment of the Old Testament's messianic promises. He lays the blame for Jesus' death squarely at feet of his hearers and then announces that this same man has been raised from the dead and vindicated as Christ. The emotional trajectory of Peter's address can be mapped not only by the response of his listeners, who are moved from perplexity and scorn to conviction, but from the verbs Luke uses to describe his preaching. Peter raises his voice to declare with urgency (Acts 2:14). He warns. He pleads (Acts 2:40). He appeals to emotion as well as to the mind.

The dynamic that is merely implied in Luke's account of Peter's preaching on the day of Pentecost is explicitly stated in his description of the conversion of Lydia. As she listened to Paul preach to the women who had gathered at the place of prayer by the river outside the city of Philippi, the Lord "opened her heart to respond to Paul's message" (Acts 16:14). Preaching is a work of the Spirit.

Can Preaching Be Taught?

Since preaching is so dependent upon the Holy Spirit, students of homiletics often wonder whether it can really be taught. If preaching is a gift—if its efficaciousness depends upon the Holy Spirit—then what need is there for the mechanics of structure or the fine points of style? These would seem to be merely extraneous factors, human additions that have the potential to complicate the simplicity of preaching and obscure God's message. Students who raise this question are quick to point out that Paul himself denounced the human artifice of Greek rhetoric.

Martyn Lloyd-Jones shared their suspicion. He considered books with titles like *The Craft of Sermon Construction* or *The Craft of Sermon Illustration* to be a prostitution of preaching and an abomination. He did not think that the act of preaching was something that could be taught. "Preachers are born, not made," Lloyd-Jones told the students of Westminster Theological Seminary. "This is an absolute. You will never teach a man to be a preacher if he is not already one. All your books such as *The A.B.C. of Preaching* or *Preaching Made Easy* should be thrown into the fire as soon as possible."[15]

It is a mistake, however, to think that training is incompatible with the work of the Holy Spirit. In Scripture, he is associated with work that involves learning and acquired skill. In Moses' day, the filling of the Holy Spirit endowed Bezaleel "with skill, ability and knowledge in all kinds of crafts" (Exod. 31:3). By the Holy Spirit, God enabled Bezaleel "to make artistic designs for work in gold, silver and bronze, to cut and set stones, to work in wood, and to engage in all kinds of craftsmanship" (Exod. 31:4–5). The Holy Spirit gave Bezaleel's assistant Oholiab similar knowledge and granted both men "the ability to teach others" (Exod. 35:34). Likewise, in Exodus 28:3 the Lord commanded "all the skilled men" to whom he had "given wisdom in such matters" to make priestly garments for Aaron.

It is reasonable to assume that this kind of ability did not come in a flash. God's artisans had to learn rudimentary skills first, probably from others, and then practice them until they became proficient. How much of this process was human and how much was the work of the Spirit? Scripture does not distinguish between the two. God's Spirit was involved not only in the exercise of these abilities once they were perfected but in their acquisition as well. "The Spirit's working shows not only in ordinary skilled labor," theologian Abraham Kuyper observes, "but also in the higher spheres of human knowledge and mental activity; for military genius, legal acumen, statesmanship, and power to inspire the masses are equally ascribed to it."[16]

Can preaching be taught? The example of Bezaleel and Oholiab suggests that the answer must be yes. God uses training to impart gifts for ministry. Not only is the Holy Spirit's work consistent with training, in the case of these Old Testament artisans at least, that training was itself an exercise of the Spirit's ministry (cf. Exod. 35:31 with 35:34). Through training, our natural abilities as speakers can be improved upon. Unintentional habits that distract our listeners can be brought under control. The student can learn about tools and techniques that enable us to analyze the text accurately and structure the sermon logically.

Still, while preaching can be taught, its effects cannot be predicted. Rhetorical methods can be learned. Skills can be acquired. We can improve our ability to communicate. But only God can determine the outcome of the sermon. The same Spirit who opens the preacher's mind to understand the text and gives utterance must work upon the mind and heart of the listener if the sermon is to produce the desired result. The preacher makes every effort to preach with skill, but dares not trust in skill alone. We can choose our words carefully. But only God can give them life.

chapter 3

THE HUMAN SIDE
OF PREACHING

Most sermons begin with prayer. Often it is a prayer which asks God to hide the preacher from view. "Let my words be forgotten, so that only what comes from you is remembered," the preacher intones. I have heard experienced pastors say this as often as students. It is easy to see why. It is a terrifying thing to take the Word of God upon your lips. Like the apostle Paul, we do not always feel that we are equal to the task. We do not want to get in God's way. We do not want to obscure the message. We do not want to embarrass ourselves or speak anything that we will have to recant later. We wonder if God might not be better served if our preaching were like the Cheshire Cat's grin. That is to say, we think it would be better if we just disappeared, so that only his Word remained.

Such prayers are well intended but misguided, if only because the first petition hardly requires an act of God. Forgetting what the preacher has said is a common occurrence among our hearers, an accomplishment which rarely necessitates divine intervention. As for the rest of the prayer, it is my contention that it misses the point. To ask God to make the preacher disappear from view fails to grasp the nature of preaching.

Preaching as a Human Word

God speaks in preaching, but through fallible human instruments whose words retain their fallible character once they have been spoken. This is one difference which separates the preached Word from the inspired words of Scripture and from prophetic utterance. We who preach are empowered by the same Spirit who spoke through the prophets and the authors of Scripture, but do not enjoy the same protection that guarded them. We declare God's Word with our own stammering tongue. We can and do err.

Sometimes our errors are errors of fact. Despite our best efforts to be accurate, we occasionally get the details wrong. At other times, our errors are those of intent. The sermon's exegesis is accurate, but its application misses the mark. And then there are those times when the error is one of tone. We say the right thing but in the wrong way. "Some speak scoldingly, and so betray their bad temper; others preach themselves, and so reveal their pride," Spurgeon warns. "Some discourse as though it were a condescension on their part to occupy the pulpit, while others preach as though they apologized for their existence."[1]

Another common error among pastors is one of dangerous familiarity with the holy. In his lectures to students at Yale, John Henry Jowett identified familiarity with the holy as an occupational hazard of preaching. "You will not have been long in the ministry before you discover that it is possible to be fussily busy about the Holy Place and yet to lose the wondering sense of the Holy Lord," Jowett warned.[2] The preacher "lives almost every hour in sight of the immensities and eternities—the awful sovereignty of God, and the glorious yet cloud-capped mysteries of redeeming grace."[3] And like those who have lived so long within view of a majestic landscape that they no longer notice its grandeur, preachers sometimes find that their own hearts have grown cold to the mysteries they declare. They speak the Word accurately but can no longer see its beauty or feel its terror.

In addition, our ability to exegete the text and analyze its structure can turn us into handlers of God's Word rather than hearers of it. We succumb to the illusion of control and falsely conclude that mastery of God's Word also gives us mastery *over* it. Or worse, we may mistakenly assume that mastery of the text means that we have been mastered *by* it. We assume that a good sermon is proof of a good life. Or we may misconstrue the tokens of success, whether measured in attendance or public acclaim, as marks of God's special favor.

This catalog of pulpit sins (which is far from exhaustive) is like a photograph which captures us in an unguarded moment and reveals our true and unflattering image. James is right to say that those who teach "stumble in many ways" (James 3:2). This might tempt us to give up the ministry of the Word altogether, if Paul's answering lament did not hold us in place: "Woe to me if I do not preach the gospel!" (1 Cor. 9:16). The apostle's cry offers a needed check to our discouraged spirit, but it is also a kind of checkmate. We cannot avoid our calling. There is a sense in which it must be said that preaching is a distinctly human enterprise. Preaching is a divine word, but it is also a human word. The heavens declare the glory of God (Ps. 19:1). The angels can preach (Matt. 28:6; Mark 16:6; Luke 24:6; Gal. 1:8; Rev. 14:6). But it is to the children of Adam that the gospel has been committed (Gal. 2:7; 1 Thess. 2:4; 1 Tim. 1:11; 6:20; 2 Tim. 1:14; Titus 1:3; Jude 1:3).

Neither can we escape our condition. The treasure that we bear has been consigned to jars of clay. We cannot help wondering at the strange wisdom which prompted God to embark on such a project. Why would God entrust such an important message to such frail messengers?

The Necessary Preacher

Perhaps it is for the same reason a jeweler chooses to set a gem in a plain setting. The stark contrast between the two natures highlights the beauty of what is most precious. Certainly God has chosen human vessels to bear this message "to show that this all-surpassing power is from God and not from us" (2 Cor. 4:7). But there is a positive reason as well. The preacher is necessary to preaching. As John Stott observes, "there is an indispensable link between the preacher and the act of preaching."[4]

God has committed his Word to human messengers because humanity is an asset when the audience you want to reach is human as well. It does not diminish the sermon to speak of it as a human word. God's use of the human is a hallmark of his work. In the incarnation of Christ, two natures were united in the one person, each without losing their fullness. The reality of the human did not detract from the divine, and the divine did not make the human more than human. Even more mysterious was God's determination to employ sinful human agents to carry out his redemptive plan. Jesus was put to death after he was handed over to "wicked men" who did what God's "power and will had decided beforehand should happen" (Acts 2:23, 4:28).

The divine and the human also work in concert in the application of Christ's work. J. I. Packer uses the term *antinomy* to describe the relationship between divine sovereignty and human responsibility in the work of evangelism. *Antinomy* refers to two things which seem to be irreconcilable yet are undeniable. "Man is a responsible moral agent, though he is *also* divinely controlled; man is divinely controlled, though he is *also* a responsible moral agent," Packer explains. "God's sovereignty is a reality, and man's responsibility is a reality too."[5]

In the written record of redemption—the inspiration of Holy Scripture—God's Spirit superintended the process but did not eclipse the personality and vocabulary of the writers. A human process resulted in a divine product. Why should we be surprised, then, to find that our humanity is also fundamental to the task of preaching? It is no wonder that in his "attempt at a new definition" of preaching, Karl Barth characterized the sermon both as "the Word of God which he himself speaks" and as "the attempt … to serve God's own Word" by expounding a biblical text.[6] According to Barth, preaching is God's own speaking, but it is also "free" speech in the sense that it is the preacher's own. "It does not consist of reading or exegesis," Barth explains. "They speak the scriptural word that they have heard, as their own independent word."[7]

We cannot hide ourselves from our listeners when we preach, no matter how hard we might try. We cannot become invisible. Nor should we want to do so. It is my contention that the preacher is necessary to preaching. When Paul asserts in 1 Corinthians 3:7 that "neither he who plants nor he who waters is anything," the obvious correlative is that the preacher is nothing. But it does not follow from this that the preacher is unnecessary. If anything, the apostle's chain of questions in Romans 10:14 implies the opposite: "How, then, can they call on the one they have not believed in? And how can they believe in the one of whom they have not heard? And how can they hear without someone preaching to them?"

For hearing to occur, there must be preaching. The Word who "didst not abhor the Virgin's womb" does not shrink from employing the human tongue to declare his Word. "You will receive power when the Holy Spirit comes on you," Jesus promised his disciples in Acts 1:8, "and you will be my witnesses in Jerusalem, and in all Judea and Samaria, and to the ends of the earth."

The role of the preacher in preaching is more than simply serving as the medium by which the content of the gospel is conveyed. "Truth through Personality is our description of real preaching," Phillips Brooks explains. "The truth must come really through the person, not merely over his lips, not merely into his understanding and out through his pen."[8] Real preaching reflects the preacher's character, affections, intellect, and moral being. When the preacher serves only as a medium for the content of the gospel, "the man has been but a printing machine or a trumpet. In the other case, he has been a true man and a real messenger of God."[9]

This means that there is more to preaching than merely projecting sounds or repeating ideas. Preaching is an exercise in communication, but it is also a kind of incarnation. During the act of preaching, the preacher serves as the living voice of the biblical text. Eugene Peterson explains why this is necessary: "Words written are radically removed from their originating context, which is the living voice. And there is far more involved in listening to a living voice than reading a written word."[10] The act of writing removes words from the living context in which they were first uttered. "Even when the context is described," Peterson explains, "the complex simultaneity of interplay and intricacy is lost. Which means that when a word is written it is reduced."[11]

We have all experienced this in exegesis when we have puzzled over the uninflected text, relying upon clues from the context and our own imagination to reanimate it, so that we might understand the author's true intent and translate it for our listeners. It is important, of course, that we not overstate this problem. It is the written word of God that Scripture describes as "living and active" (Heb. 4:12). What is more, much of the Bible was written down before it was spoken aloud to God's people. This was true of much of the law of Moses (Exod. 24:7; Deut. 31:11). It was certainly true of the New Testament epistles.

Yet it is significant that in most cases the first encounter of God's people with the Scriptures was in oral rather than written form. The written word of God was read aloud to the congregation, an oral experience that was facilitated through the living voice of someone other than the human author (Josh. 8:35; 2 Kings 23:2; Neh. 8:8, 18; Col. 4:16; 1 Thess. 5:27). Even if this had not been the case with the audience to whom these documents were originally addressed, it certainly would have been true of subsequent generations. This kind of public reading, as Stephen H. Webb points out, is by its very nature an interpretive act: "The inflection of one's voice determines the meaning of words written on a page."[12]

Inflecting the Text

Consequently, preaching is by its very nature an exercise in inflection. This involves more than pitch, volume, and tone. In the sermon, the preacher makes God's written word incarnate by speaking the biblical author's words into the contemporary context. This is an inflection of the text itself, a responsibility which places a dual obligation upon the preacher. One dimension of the preacher's responsibility is to the text itself. The preacher's aim in the sermon is to animate the text without altering it. The written word has been detached from its original context but is not freed from it. The fact that we must speak to circumstances that the biblical writers did not originally envision does not give us liberty to wrest the Scriptures from their original context and make them say whatever we please.

The other area of responsibility is to the audience. An uninflected text is a dead text as far as the listener is concerned. "Somehow or other, every other agency dealing with the public recognizes that contact with the actual life of the auditor is the one place to begin," Harry Emerson Fosdick chided preachers during the early part of the twentieth century. "Only the preacher proceeds still upon the idea that folk come to church desperately anxious to discover what happened to the Jebusites."[13] It is possible that Fosdick's point has been heeded too well by contemporary preachers. But this does not make his assessment less true.

However, preachers cannot afford to ignore what happened to the Jebusites, any more than they can afford to overlook those who are present as the sermon is being delivered. A sermon which focuses only on the concerns of the contemporary audience and pays no attention to the historical and literary context of Scripture co-opts the text instead of inflecting it, turning the living and active Word into a ventriloquist's dummy. Such preaching is little more than a caricature whose hollow voice merely echoes the preacher's own thinking.

Still, Fosdick's complaint must be reckoned with. Even the apostle Paul acknowledges the distance that can exist between the concerns of the text and those of the audience when he uses the Old Testament law that forbade the muzzling of oxen as an analogy in 1 Corinthians 9:9–10. If it is true that the folk who come to church are not especially anxious to learn what happened to the Jebusites, they are even less interested in the oxen that plowed the land the Jebusites once inhabited. Paul gives voice to the fundamental question of the audience when he cites what the law says about oxen and then declares in 1 Corinthians 9:10, "Surely he says this for us, doesn't he?" The answer is yes, according to the apostle. And no wonder, "For everything that was written in the past was written to teach us, so that through endurance and the encouragement of the Scriptures we might have hope" (Rom. 15:4). The historical particularity of the biblical text is not an obstacle to the relevance of the sermon.

Despite this assurance, the connection between what was said and what must be said is not always direct. Nor is it always obvious. The law of oxen does not necessarily translate into "Four Secrets to Successful Farming." Even if it did, not all who hear us would be farmers. Principles must be extrapolated and implications drawn for the contemporary listener. This is hard work, at least as difficult as the work of exegesis. It is, in fact, the counterpart to exegesis. It is this work which gives biblical revelation what David Wells describes as its "bipolar" nature. Scripture is bipolar in the sense that it has a point of origin and a destination point. Biblical revelation's point of origin is the context in which it was given. The destination point is the contemporary context. The task of the theology, according to Wells, is "to discover what God has said in and through Scripture and then to clothe that in a conceptuality which is native to our own age."[14]

We find a good example of the kind of trajectory Wells is talking about in the directive Moses gave for the public reading of the law in Deuteronomy 31:10–13. According to the command, this reading was to take place every seven years, "when all Israel comes to appear before the LORD your God at the place he will choose" (v. 11). This envisioned Israel not only as already settled in the land but as having been settled there for multiple cycles of seven years. Yet Moses issued the command while Israel was still encamped on the plains of Moab, before they had even crossed the Jordan. In other words, Moses' command was addressed to subsequent generations, as much as it was to those who were within earshot.

This forward motion reflects the general trajectory of all biblical revelation. Biblical revelation belongs "to us and to our children forever" (Deut. 29:29). To make this journey, Scripture must be decontextualized and recontextualized. Consequently, Wells explains, "The biblical revelation, because of its inspired nature, can therefore be captive neither to the culture in which it arose nor to the culture in which it arrives."[15] This process of decontextualization, extrapolation into transcultural principles, and then recontextualization is the preacher's main work. The Holy Spirit provides insight for the task but does not deliver us from its necessity. It is our job to synthesize the exegetical data into a message which is suited to the lives of those who hear the message. It is this work of application which gives the sermon its distinctive voice by putting a face on the biblical text for the listener.

In fact, the sermon, like the cherubim who appeared to the prophet Ezekiel, actually presents four faces to the audience. One is the face of God, who speaks through his Word. Another is the face of the biblical text, human words addressed by the author to a human audience whose immediate circumstances may have been radically different from our own. The third face is the face of the listener, who must see himself both as he is and as he might be by God's grace as a result of the truth of the text. Yet none of this erases the face of the preacher, whose work and personality serve as the sermon's living voice. Like it or not, we cannot hide ourselves from view. We cannot make ourselves invisible and still fulfill our calling as preachers.

Preaching Ourselves

Scot McKnight writes of an exercise he does with his students in his course on Jesus of Nazareth. On the opening day of class, he gives them a standardized psychological test divided into two parts. On the first part, the students describe Jesus' personality. On the second, they compare their own personality with Jesus. "The test is not about right or wrong answers, nor is it designed to help students understand Jesus," McKnight explains. "Instead, if given to enough people, the test will reveal that we all think Jesus is like us. Introverts think Jesus is introverted, for example, and, on the basis of the same questions, extroverts think Jesus is extroverted."[16]

McKnight appeals to this tendency to make a point about the search for the "historical" Jesus. But his example also raises a question of preaching. If one of our functions as preachers is to put a face on the biblical text, how do we avoid recasting the text into our own image? The answer is that we are not meant to avoid this. At least, not entirely. It is true that we preach Christ and not ourselves. But this does not mean that we should remove ourselves from the message. "For we do not preach ourselves, but Jesus Christ as Lord," Paul explains, "and ourselves as your servants for Jesus' sake" (2 Cor. 4:5). We do not preach ourselves, and yet we do.

Writers often use the metaphor of "voice" to speak of an author's personality and unique point of view. Preaching too is concerned with voice, both in this literary as well as in a more literal sense. In the sermon, the preacher gives voice to the text by providing a contextualized understanding of the passage. This is the result of insight afforded by the Holy Spirit through the preacher's study. But it is also an insight which is mediated to the audience through the preacher. In other words, the unique gift that the preacher brings to the sermon is the filter of his own personality and experience.

In a sermon on the white stone and new name of Revelation 2:17, George MacDonald describes each person as having both an individual relationship with God and a unique relation to God: "He is to God a peculiar being, made after his own fashion, and that of no one else; for when he is perfected he shall receive the new name which no one else can understand."[17] For MacDonald, this meant that each person is blessed with a distinctive angle of vision when it comes to understanding God: "Hence, he can worship God as no man else can worship him, can understand God as no man else can understand him. This or that man may understand God more, may understand God better than he, but no other man can understand God *as* he understands him."[18]

If MacDonald is right, every preacher speaks with a distinct voice and provides a unique perspective into God and his Word. The sermon is not a bare restatement of the text. It is a reflection on the text after it has passed through the experience and personality of the preacher. It is an embodied truth. This personal element means that the best preaching is marked by a kind of homiletical nakedness. Dynamic preaching gives listeners the sense that they know God through the preacher. But this privilege of incarnating the message is also a responsibility. Properly harnessed and appropriately expressed, such self-disclosure can be disarming. When it is mishandled, it distorts the sermon the way a gaudy frame distracts the viewer's attention from the picture it is meant to accent.

The margin of error between incarnation and self-absorption is narrower than a razor's edge. There is only one tether strong enough to keep the preacher from slipping from appropriate self-disclosure into narcissism. That is the anchor of God's truth. It is only by giving careful attention to the message of Scripture that we are able to rein in our natural bent toward self-absorption. Paul is right after all. We do not preach ourselves. We preach Christ.

chapter 4

PREACHING
AND AUTHORITY

Not long after I graduated from seminary, I spoke to a friend about my discouragement with the church I was serving. Looking back, I realize now that things were not as bad as they appeared. The opposition I faced was the sort that every young pastor deals with, especially when he is eager to prove himself. But at the time, it seemed to me that I had made a terrible mistake by accepting a call to this congregation. Some of the charter members were grumbling about changes I had initiated. A few even hinted that I had bullied the church's leaders into seeing things my way. The displeasure they felt was evident to me as I preached. Their criticism was unfounded, but it stung just the same. I wondered whether I should tender my resignation and look for another congregation that would be more responsive to my leadership. My friend listened to this tale of woe in silence. At last he replied, "Worse things have been said about better men."

Jesus promised that those who speak in his name will also share in his reproach: "A student is not above his teacher, nor a servant above his master. It is enough for the student to be like his teacher, and the servant like his master. If the head of the house has been called Beelzebub, how much more the members of his household!" (Matt. 10:24–25). Preaching with divine authority does not guarantee a smooth path. We would like to think that God-given authority gives us leverage. "Listen to us," we want to say to our audience. "We speak for God." But the same Bible that gives us our authority also offers ample proof of the congregation's capacity for discounting that authority.

A Question of Authority

The question of authority affects both sides of the pulpit. How does a preacher dare to stand before the congregation and declare "thus saith the Lord"? Preaching seems presumptuous, especially in an age when truth is relative and the veracity of the Bible is no longer presupposed. For the audience, the preacher's authority is a question of validity. They want to know why they should take us at our word. They have good reason to doubt. Ours is not the only voice that cries to them from the wilderness. Today's listener lives in a world where kings and queens are merely figureheads and where authority is treated as if it were a synonym for authoritarianism. They are justifiably suspicious of anyone who claims to speak with final authority.

It is not only our authority as preachers that contemporary listeners challenge but the very concept of authority itself. "Of late, the whole idea of authority has been shaken; it totters," David Buttrick observes.[1] "Traditional Protestantism rests on a working model of authority involving Word and Spirit, but the synthesis of Word and Spirit has collapsed, torn apart by cultural splits between reason and feeling, between so-called objective and subjective truth ... We wrestle not with particular notions of 'authority' but with the whole authority model per se."[2] Despite these doubts, the preacher does not have the liberty to cast authority aside as if it were a curious artifact from a bygone age whose function we longer comprehend. Authority is inherent to the very nature of preaching. There is no such thing as unauthoritative preaching.

Authority is also necessary for the preacher's confidence. Preaching is an awkward business. Those who preach do not give advice; they declare. They tell the congregation what is right and what is wrong. When God's people turn to the right or the left, the preacher stands before them like the angel who stood in Balaam's path, and says, "This is the way; walk in it." What right do we have to make such demands? Who are we to tell others how to live?

Preaching is impolite. When we preach, we often draw public conclusions about the motives of our listeners and impugn their character. We utter things from the pulpit that we would not dare to say in private conversation, at least not to strangers! We tell our listeners things about themselves that they would be offended to hear from the teller at the bank or from their doctor, even when such things are true. Indeed, they are not always happy to hear them from us. Where do we find the nerve to say what must be said? The answer, in a word, is authority.

All Authority Is Given

There is no need to apologize for speaking with authority when we preach, because we do not speak for ourselves. The authority to which we appeal is derived authority. When Jesus commanded his disciples to baptize and teach, he linked their commission with his own. "All authority in heaven and on earth has been given to me," Jesus told them. "Therefore go and make disciples of all nations, baptizing them in the name of the Father and of the Son and of the Holy Spirit, and teaching them to obey everything I have commanded you" (Matt. 28:18–20). These are sweeping claims. Jesus claims not some authority but all authority, not only authority in heaven but authority on earth. Jesus is master of his domain and master of ours as well.

This is not the first mention Scripture makes of Jesus' authority. Christ's authority was evident throughout his earthly ministry. Those who heard him were amazed by his teaching, "because he taught as one who had authority, and not as their teachers of the law" (Matt. 7:29). He told his opponents that he possessed "authority on earth to forgive sins," a prerogative which belongs to God alone (Matt. 9:6). Jesus also said he had "authority over all people" (John 17:2). Yet the authority which Jesus claims in these verses is itself derived authority. It is authority which "has been given" (Matt. 28:18). In the Great Commission, Jesus reaffirms his universal authority and invests his disciples with it.

If Jesus was not ashamed to point beyond himself for the authority of his words, we should not be ashamed to do so either. Whatever confidence we may have in preaching, it is not self-confidence. But neither should we regard the authority we have received from Christ as a talisman which guarantees a positive response from our listeners. Indeed, given Jesus' experience, one cannot help wondering how the disciples took any encouragement from his words. The genuineness of Jesus' authority did not make the religious leaders any more receptive to his messianic claims. The astonishment of the crowd did not keep them from turning their backs. Jesus' example is proof enough that authority, even when it is divine, does not guarantee obedience.

The fact that those who hear us can and do resist God's authority does not make them any less accountable to God. Just because they can say no does not mean that they should. It does suggest that it may be as much for our sake as for the sake of those to whom we preach that Jesus grounds the Great Commission in his own authority. Divine authority binds the preacher to the message as well as to the audience. We are not like the Sophists, paid philosophers whose primary aim was to delight those who heard them. We are not entertainers or even motivational speakers. The weight of Christ's authority adds weight to our words. It propels us forward in our mission. But it also places a burden of obligation upon us. We are heralds of the Risen King. We do not speak for ourselves. Woe to us if we do not preach the gospel.

This is the preacher's prophetic responsibility. "Prophetic preaching does not necessarily imply that the preacher assumes the role of Jeremiah or Amos, but that the preacher remains faithful to the prophetic dimensions of biblical texts," Thomas G. Long explains. "If the word comes from God in the biblical text, the preacher remains true to that word, regardless of the reaction or the cost."[3]

The Authority of the Text

Consequently, preaching derives its primary authority from the text of Scripture. Our work of correcting, rebuking, and encouraging flows from a more fundamental command: "Preach the Word" (2 Tim. 4:2). There are some who prefer to point past the text and locate the preacher's authority in the ideas of Scripture, generally in the gospel or more particularly in the person of Christ. David Buttrick, for example, writes, "Of course, when we claim that the Bible is our 'authority,' we are pointing past texts, and past even the gospel in scripture, to God-for-us in Jesus Christ."[4]

Buttrick is right to say that the Scriptures point beyond themselves to Christ. Jesus asserted as much when he told the religious leaders, "You diligently study the Scriptures because you think that by them you possess eternal life. These are the Scriptures that testify about me, yet you refuse to come to me to have life" (John 5:39–40). But Jesus also testified to the authority of the biblical text, down to the smallest letter and the least stroke of the pen (Matt. 5:18). He said that Scripture cannot be broken (John 10:35).

It is certainly possible to misunderstand the Scriptures. We can intentionally twist them. But we cannot put Jesus at odds with the authority of the text of Scripture without putting Jesus at odds with himself. To attribute authority to Christ but to deny it to the Scriptures is a contradiction. The Scriptures testify about Christ, and Christ bears witness to the Scriptures. Each speaks of the other, and they both speak with the same voice.

Buttrick is also right when he says that there is a relationship between the authority of the sermon and hermeneutics. He identifies this as the question which has shaken the Christian idea of authority to its core: "Basically, the hermeneutical question is *the* question."[5] Preachers do not always agree when it comes to interpreting the Scriptures. They especially do not agree about the implications a passage may have for today's audience. Buttrick observes, "Let fifty preachers loose with the same passage from scripture and we can safely expect at least a dozen different distillations of 'God's Word.' It is all very well to castigate poor preachers for (sneer!) deplorable eisegesis; frequently preachers earn the rebuke but, to be honest, the meaning of texts *now* is difficult to discern."[6]

The authority of the sermon is indeed a function of hermeneutics, but the authority of the biblical text is not. Illegitimate hermeneutics robs the sermon of its authority, but it cannot diminish the authority of the text. A misinterpreted text is still an authoritative text. The interpreter's distortion may carry no weight, but the text continues to bear the weight of its inherent authority. Indeed, if the text were not authoritative in its own right, we would not care whether the preacher's interpretation is the right one. Our anxiety over "the hermeneutical question" is itself an implicit recognition that the text speaks with authority. The Scriptures do not depend upon our recognition or even our understanding for their authority.

"Accordingly, we must here remember that whatever authority and dignity the Spirit in Scripture accords to either priests or prophets, or apostles, or successors of apostles, it is wholly given not to the men personally, but to the ministry to which they have been appointed; or (to speak more briefly) to the Word, whose ministry is entrusted to them," Calvin reminds us. "For if we examine them all in order, we shall not find that they have been endowed with any authority to teach or to answer, except in the name and Word of the Lord."[7]

In saying this Calvin points to a fundamental difference between the Reformers and the Roman Catholic Church. Both believed that the church was vested with authority. "Our opponents locate the authority of the church outside God's Word," Calvin argued, "but we insist that it be attached to the Word, and do not allow it to be separated from it."[8] The church is under the Word, and because it is under the Word, the preacher's authority flows from the Word. Eliminate the authority of the text and you also eliminate all grounds for the sermon's authority.

The Authority of Experience

Experience verifies the truth of what the preacher says. Often this experiential authority functions by way of analogy. Analogy is a mirror that reflects the listeners' experience back to them. But it is also a window, enabling hearers to look through their known experience to discover what is as yet unknown. Jesus appeals to experience by way of analogy in Luke 11:11 – 13 when he asks, "Which of you fathers, if your son asks for a fish, will give him a snake instead? Or if he asks for an egg, will give him a scorpion? If you then, though you are evil, know how to give good gifts to your children, how much more will your Father in heaven give the Holy Spirit to those who ask him!" Do Jesus' words imply that we do not know God? Or is he saying that we know God better than we think? Either way, the point of comparison is our own experience, arguing from the lesser to the greater.

The Bible often invites us to experience new realities when it calls us to act in terms of the metaphors and analogies that describe the spiritual realities of the gospel. This is the line of reasoning Paul employs in Romans 6:1 – 3 when he asks, "What shall we say, then? Shall we go on sinning so that grace may increase? By no means! We died to sin; how can we live in it any longer? Or don't you know that all of us who were baptized into Christ Jesus were baptized into his death?" In Romans 6:20 – 21, Paul appeals to past experience to ignite the motivational energy necessary for following through with this call to live as those who have died to sin: "When you were slaves to sin, you were free from the control of righteousness. What benefit did you reap at that time from the things you are now ashamed of? Those things result in death!" These are all arguments from experience.

This relationship between language and experience is fundamental to understanding and communicating truth about God. "A Paul or an Augustine understands his life in some sense as a metaphor of his theology and his theology as a metaphor of his life," Sallie McFague TeSelle explains. "Life and thought mutually illuminate each other: I come to understand what I believe and the language I use only as I live it, and I am able to live my belief and the language I use only as I come to understand them more clearly."[9] No wonder Jesus marveled to Nicodemus in John 3:12, "I have spoken to you of earthly things and you do not believe; how then will you believe if I speak of heavenly things?"

The effects of God's Word upon those who believe offer further proof from experience. J. Gresham Machen calls this "one of the primary evidences for the truth of the gospel record" and notes, "Salvation does depend upon what happened long ago, but the event of long ago has effects that continue today."[10] This line of authority appeals to Christian experience for evidence of the truth of God's Word. It corroborates the truth of the biblical text but cannot stand in its place. Machen explains, "Christian experience is rightly used when it helps to convince us that events narrated in the New Testament actually did occur; but it can never enable us to be Christians whether the events occurred or not."[11]

The Authority of Ethos

The authority of our message must go beyond words. It must also be supported by the experience of the preacher. This personal argument for the truth of the text has traditionally been called the ethos of the sermon. Ethos is the silent but visible language of character which offers living proof of the transforming power of God's Word. The biblical term used to describe this dimension of proclamation is *witness*. When the disciples hoped to be elevated to kingdom authority soon after Christ's resurrection, Jesus promised them a different kind of power: "It is not for you to know the times or dates the Father has set by his own authority. But you will receive power when the Holy Spirit comes on you; and you will be my witnesses in Jerusalem, and in all Judea and Samaria, and to the ends of the earth" (Acts 1:7–8).

A witness is someone who speaks from experience. But there is also a forensic quality to this metaphor. When the Bible speaks of witnesses, it usually mentions them in connection with a trial. A witness is someone who offers personal experience as evidence. Thomas G. Long thinks that the legal cast to this metaphor is one reason it does not appeal to many homileticians. "An aura of law and judgment surrounds the witness idea," Long explains, "and this appears to be at odds with the grace and freedom associated with preaching the gospel."[12]

Nevertheless, the forensic tone of the witness metaphor has important implications for preaching. This responsibility of bearing witness gives the preacher's words a bipolar quality. A witness can testify for or against someone, functioning as advocate or accuser. If the witness appears on my behalf, they act as my advocate. If the witness testifies against me, they act as my accuser. Often the witness occupies both roles at the same time. By speaking on one person's behalf, they bear witness against someone else. As a herald of the gospel and a teacher of God's Word, the preacher gives testimony on behalf of Christ but against those who are in need of the gospel's grace. This is because the gospel's promise comes with an implicit accusation. Jesus' answer to the religious leaders when they asked why he ate with tax collectors and sinners reflects this: "On hearing this, Jesus said to them, 'It is not the healthy who need a doctor, but the sick. I have not come to call the righteous, but sinners'" (Mark 2:17). By declaring the gospel to our audience, we imply that they are guilty sinners who are in need of God's grace.

At the same time, by proclaiming the grace of the gospel, the preacher engages in a ministry of advocacy toward the congregation. The gospel's accusation is tendered in the form of an invitation. To use Jesus' metaphor, the gospel is a doctor in search of the sick. Only sinners need apply here. Preaching is a form of advocacy which seeks to reconcile God and sinners: "We are therefore Christ's ambassadors, as though God were making his appeal through us. We implore you on Christ's behalf: Be reconciled to God" (2 Cor. 5:20).

But the sinner is not the only one who is on trial when God's Word is proclaimed. Preaching is a declaration, but it is also a defense (Phil. 1:16). The one who preaches is also under scrutiny. Under the law of Moses, as in our own court system, anyone who gave testimony was subject to "thorough investigation" (Deut. 19:18). The preacher who bears witness to God's Word is just as liable to undergo a rigorous cross-examination. Paul was not ashamed to implore others on Christ's behalf. He appealed to his own way of life as well as to Scripture (Acts 26:4). The content of our preaching is important. But the rigors of cross-examination demand that we keep an eye on ourselves as well as our doctrine (1 Tim. 4:16).

"We must assiduously attend to the culture of our souls" if our words are to have the ring of authority.[13] The old word for this kind of attention is *piety*. It is a word that has fallen out of favor in our day. Call someone pious today and you slander them. You might as well call them a Pharisee or a hypocrite. It does not matter very much that the word has fallen out of use. It is the loss of the practice that should concern us.

We should not, however, attribute to ethos a power in the sermon which belongs to God alone. Ethos can amplify the preacher's message, but it cannot serve as a substitute for the authority of the biblical text. Good ethos is not a guarantee of good results. Godly preachers like Jeremiah are sometimes ignored, while surly and self-centered preachers like Jonah may be heeded beyond all expectation.

Nor can the words of affirmation which we crave so much from the audience be trusted. The same hands that build monuments to the prophets and lay wreaths upon their graves also have the power to shed the prophet's blood (Matt. 23:29; Luke 11:51). Not many of us will be slain between the altar and the sanctuary like Zechariah, but many of our sermons have suffered a similar fate as a result of the rough treatment they received between the church parking lot and the lunch table.

We wear the prophetic mantle, but not a bulletproof vest. The preaching office does not shield us from unfair criticism, petty complaint, or bitter invective. Neither does it guarantee that every barb thrust at us is falsely aimed. Some of the complaints leveled against us are all the more bitter because we know they are true. Sadly, the reproach we bear is not always the reproach of Christ. My friend was right. Worse things have been said about better people. And sometimes better things are said about us than we deserve.

chapter 5

SPEAKING FOR
THE SILENT GOD

God has a voice. His is a great thundering voice. God's voice cracks like a bolt from the sky, sharp enough to split the cedars. A hurricane blast that strips bare all that lies within its path, it rattles the bones of the earth (Psalm 29). His is also a small voice, tiny as the piping of a sparrow. Tender as a mother's caress, its murmur is softer than silence. When God speaks, he whispers with gentle insistence, the way a parent might stir a sleeping child (1 Kings 19:12; 1 Sam. 3:4–11).

God has a voice.

But he rarely uses it.

You would not think so, to hear some people talk. God, as they describe him, is a garrulous deity, a constant chatterer who carries on a running conversation day and night. I have even known some who claimed to have spoken to him face to face. They say he appeared to them in a dream or sat down by their bedside. But such a thing has never happened to me. It has not happened to most of the Christians

I know, even though we pray, "Speak, Lord, for your servant is listening." Like the boy Samuel, we lie in our beds and wait. But there is no answering reply.

Although I have never heard God's voice, I see the evidence of its existence every day. The presence of the physical world is proof that God has a voice. The heavens and the earth that we see exist because God spoke them into being (Gen. 1:3).The beauty of creation has prompted humankind to speculate about God from earliest memory. The *Enuma Elish*, an ancient Babylonian creation account, is a good example of this. "To the people who told and heard this epic," Andy Crouch observes, "it must have seemed obvious that the world needed a story ... This is what human beings do: we extract stories from the stars."[1]

But according to the Scriptures, the stars tell their own story. The heavens engage in a continuous narrative about God (Ps. 19:1 – 2). By their expanse, they "proclaim the work of his hands." They employ a universal language and speak in a voice that is heard in "all the earth" (v. 4). The shout that the psalmist depicts as ringing in the vault of the heavens is not the echo of God's first word but creation's antiphonal reply. It is the testimony of creation that reveals "what may be known about God" (Rom. 1:19 – 20). This is not an audible cry but a kind of sign language, a visual monologue which discloses what would otherwise remain hidden about God. "As a consequence," Calvin says, "men cannot open their eyes without being compelled to see him."[2] This visible testimony reveals God's invisible qualities. Through creation, God's eternal power and divine nature are "clearly seen." Creation does not provide the details of God's redemptive plan, but it is enough to leave humanity without excuse.

Despite the eloquence and the clarity of what creation can tell us about God, we long for an audible word. Yet God does not speak to us directly. Some of us are vexed by this, offended by God the way we might be by a neighbor who refuses to speak to us over the fence. Yet silence is such a common characteristic of the way God deals with humanity that the Bible always takes special notice when that silence is broken. The truth is, as far as his audible voice is concerned, God keeps silent far more than he chooses to speak. His common practice is exemplified in the sentiment of Proverbs 27:2: "Let another praise you, and not your own mouth; someone else, and not your own lips." God rarely uses his own voice but prefers to let others speak for him. This is the singular glory of preaching. Those who preach break God's silence.

Why Is God Silent?

Theologian Helmut Thielicke describes God's silence as an objective thing: "Even the angels who stand about the throne of God can testify that God's silence is real; so far is it from being merely a figment of man's deluded and hardened heart. God really can be silent."[3] What are we to make of this? If God can speak, why doesn't he?

Silence is a reflection of God's transcendent nature and is linked with his invisibility in Scripture. Jesus contrasted the experience of Moses — one who heard God's voice and spoke face to face with him — with that of his enemies in John 5:37: "You have never heard his voice nor seen his form." Yet even Moses did not see God in his essence but was merely granted a limited vision of God's goodness, coupled with the proclamation of his name (Exod. 33:19). The Lord himself described what Moses saw as his "back" (v. 23). This was for Moses' sake, since no one can see God and live (v. 20).

According to hymn writer Walter Chalmers Smith, the immortal, invisible God is "silent as light." Smith's description echoes the language of the apostle Paul in 1 Timothy 1:17, which describes God as eternal, immortal, and invisible.[4] Theologians disagree over what believers will finally see when they are in God's presence, yet all agree that in our present experience, he remains unseen as far as his essence is concerned.

God is also silent by intention. In some cases this silence anticipates judgment. When the seventh seal is opened in the book of

Revelation, the first thing to issue from it is not the rolling thunder of the saints' prayers or the earth-shattering blast of the seven trumpets but a silence that is the prelude to judgment (Rev. 8:1). In other instances, silence *is* the judgment. Most children know this instinctively and dread the disapproving silence of a loving parent far more than they do the sting of open rebuke. God "by no means judges merely—or better, he hardly ever judges by smiting the transgressor with a stroke of lightning or some other disaster; on the contrary he judges him by letting him go in silence."[5]

Silence was the evidence that God's favor had been removed from Saul and rested on David (1 Sam. 28:6). In the same way, David pleaded with God not to leave him in silence, comparing the silence of God to the silence of death. When God's voice is unheard, we are like those who "have gone down to the pit" (Ps. 28:1). Elsewhere, the psalmist compares divine silence to deafness. He fears divine silence because it implies that God has been deaf to his cry for help (Ps. 39:12). Israel learned to connect these two things through bitter experience, when God turned a "deaf ear" to their weeping after the rebellion at Kadesh Barnea (Deut. 1:45).

But it is Jesus who offers the most decisive proof of the connection between divine silence and judgment. First, his refusing to answer his critics and his silence before Pilate were a kind of judgment (Mark 11:33; John 19:9). Then his terrible question uttered from the cross: "My God, my God, why have you forsaken me?" This was a cry aimed at the descending silence more than the surrounding darkness. By claiming the words of Psalm 22 as his own, Jesus identifies with the psalmist's experience of divine silence: "O my God, I cry out by day, but you do not answer" (Ps. 22:2). Divine silence is an act of judgment, which means that silence is itself a statement.

Silence as an Act of Grace

At the same time, God's silence can be an expression of his grace. This, in fact, may be one of the keys to understanding why God rarely speaks to us in an audible voice. God chose to address his people indirectly through the prophets in response to Israel's own request. Scripture records that they could not bear to hear the voice of God (Deut. 18:16; cf. Exod. 20:19). The experience so terrified them, they "begged that no further word be spoken to them" (Heb. 12:19).

Israel's encounter was proof "that a man can live even if God speaks with him" (Deut. 5:24). Yet their request that future communication come through a human mediator was rooted in the fear that they could not survive if God continued to address them directly. "But now, why should we die? This great fire will consume us, and we will die if we hear the voice of the LORD our God any longer," they reasoned. "For what mortal man has ever heard the voice of the living God speaking out of fire, as we have, and survived?" (Deut. 5:25–26).

No doubt the loud volume, fire, cloud, and deep darkness that accompanied God's voice contributed to the terror of the moment. But their fear was rooted in what God had said even more than how he said it. They begged God to speak no further "because they could not bear what was commanded" (Heb. 12:20). In particular, they were terrified by the warning that anyone who touched the mountain would be put to death (Exod. 19:12–13). The solution, proposed by Israel and graciously accepted by God, was to introduce a third party into the communication loop. God would speak to Moses, and Moses would speak to Israel on God's behalf.

This concession anticipated the birth of the prophetic office in the life of Israel. Moses became the first in a long line of human representatives to speak for God.[6] Yet Moses' experience was singular when compared with that of the prophets. The Lord made this clear when an argument erupted with Miriam and Aaron over Moses' role. The dispute was sparked not by anything Moses said but by his decision to marry a Cushite (Num. 12:1–8). Miriam and Aaron complained, "Has the LORD spoken only through Moses? Hasn't he also spoken through us?" The connection between this reasoning and Moses' marriage is unclear. Maybe they felt they needed a spiritual reason to criticize the union. Perhaps they were two separate issues. It is even possible that their disagreement with the marriage was merely a pretext that allowed them to raise the real thing that bothered them: the jealousy they felt over Moses' authority.

Whatever the rationale, the Lord's response emphasized the uniqueness of Moses' experience compared with other prophets. To others, the Lord revealed himself in visions and dreams, "But this is not true of my servant Moses; he is faithful in all my house. With him I speak face to face, clearly and not in riddles; he sees the form of the LORD" (Num. 12:7–8). This was the divine response to Miriam's criticism. It was true that God did not speak only *through* Moses. But he did speak directly only *to* Moses. Miriam and Aaron had not had the same experience that Moses had. Indeed, Moses' own description of his experience underscores the difference between them: "The LORD would speak to Moses face to face, as a man speaks with his friend" (Exod. 33:11).

Silence as Exclamation

God's silence does not mean that he is absent or disengaged. Silence can be as much a feature of presence as it is of absence. Job's three friends were as present in their silence as they were in their speech (Job 2:13). Indeed, it might be said that they were more present in their silence because they stopped being listeners when they opened their mouths to speak. The silence of Job's friends was far more comforting to the troubled patriarch than their words, as evidenced by Job's complaint, "How long will you torment me and crush me with words?" (Job 19:2).

God, of course, does not suffer from the limited perspective of Job's friends. He does not misinterpret circumstances or speak rashly. If he were to speak, he would say just the right thing. But the misguided speech of Job's failed comforters is ample proof that silent listening is also a feature of presence and may be more comforting than words. God is present when he is silent.

Silence, therefore, is not synonymous with emptiness. In music, the rests are as essential to the rhythm as the musical notes. Silence is one of the elements a composer uses to move the piece forward. Jeremy Begbie asks, "Why are we so petrified of silence? Presumably because we think nothing happens in silence. But music's metrical waves extend even through silence. We can sense them even when there is no music."[7] God uses silence to make us aware of his presence.

Silence is equally important in public speaking, in which a pause can be as important as what is said. When a speaker pauses intentionally during delivery, the space between words focuses the listener's attention. What is more, the power of a silent pause is bidirectional. A pause has as much power to create anticipation for what is about to be said as it does to underscore what was just said.

Power of the pause

This explains the long silences of God. In the Bible, remarkable instances of God's speaking are separated by extended periods when there is no word from the Lord. These years of silence served to concentrate the attention of God's people on what God had already said, even as they created a longing to hear what he would say next. Silence is God's exclamation point.

As the age of the patriarchs drew to a close in the book of Genesis, Joseph reiterated God's earlier promise, spoken directly to Abraham, that God would bring their descendants out of Egypt and restore them to the land of Canaan (Gen. 50:24; cf. 15:12–14). Joseph's reminder was followed by four hundred years of silence. When Jehovah finally broke his silence, he took pains to reassure Moses that he had remembered both God's people and his promises in the interim (Exod. 3:6–10). The long silence paved the way for Moses' ministry as God's messenger.

Moses in turn predicted the coming of "a prophet like me," anticipating the rise of the prophetic ministry in Israel (Deut. 18:15). Yet after Moses' death, a silence ensued that lasted approximately three hundred years, during which "the word of the LORD was rare" (1 Sam. 3:1). This silence was broken with a whisper, when the Lord spoke directly to Samuel and inaugurated the age of the Old Testament prophets. Another silence lasting nearly four hundred years separates the last promise uttered by the last prophet in the Old Testament canon and the birth of John the Baptist. As the fulfillment of Malachi's prophecy that God would send "the prophet Elijah" before the great and terrible day of the Lord and as forerunner to the Messiah, John served as a kind of bridge between the Old Testament prophets and Jesus Christ, the one whom the whole prophetic line anticipated (Mal. 4:5; Matt. 11:14; Rev. 19:10).

Since the close of the canon, the church has experienced a silence which has lasted for nearly two millennia. Peter's warning that the church take care not to misinterpret the apparent delay in Christ's return seems to anticipate something like this. He exhorts the church to look back to "the words spoken in the past by the holy prophets and the command given by our Lord and Savior through your apostles" (2 Peter 3:2). If silence serves as God's exclamation point, then we should not be surprised: "In the past God spoke to our forefathers through the prophets at many times and in various ways, but in these last days he has spoken to us by his Son, whom he appointed heir of all things, and through whom he made the universe" (Heb. 1:1–2). Jesus is God in the flesh, the Father's agent in creation and his final word to humanity. When the writer of Hebrews emphasizes the frequency with which God has spoken to his people and the variety of ways he has done so, he underscores the singular nature of God's revelation of himself in Jesus Christ. "In these last days" God has revealed himself definitively through Jesus Christ. Jesus is God's final word about himself. All that needs to be said about God has been summed up in the person and work of Jesus Christ because he is God in the flesh.

This does not diminish the importance of God's written revelation. We would not know Christ apart from the Scriptures. Jesus Christ is God's final word in the sense that he is at the center of all biblical revelation. The Old Testament anticipated Christ's arrival. The Gospels describe his advent. The Epistles spell out the implications of his suffering, and the book of Revelation depicts the events that surround his return. The book of Revelation, the Bible's last prophetic book, states that "the testimony of Jesus is the spirit of prophecy" (Rev. 19:10). The Bible addresses a variety of subjects. It recounts the history of God's people and describes their experience of God. It contains beautiful poetry and offers sound wisdom for ordering our lives. But its single unifying theme is Christ.

The silence of this age is an exclamatory silence. God has stopped talking because all that needs to be said has been summed up in the person of Christ. Those who preach do not come with a new word. Instead, they declare and apply that which has already been said. Like the apostle Paul, the preacher's message is shaped by a determination to "know nothing ... except Jesus Christ and him crucified" (1 Cor. 2:2).

The Fundamental Assumption of Preaching

The fundamental theological assumption of preaching is that the preacher speaks for God. Admittedly, this is a view that has fallen somewhat out of favor in recent days. Many homileticians claim that today's preachers have lost the authoritative base they once enjoyed. David Buttrick observes, "The glow is gone from the gilt-edged page, the glint from the shepherd's crook. The unassailable fact that faces us today is a dramatic, perhaps inevitable collapse of authority."[8]

Buttrick argues that this collapse is the result of a crisis in hermeneutics. The cultural distance between today's audience and those addressed by the original text, combined with significant interpretive differences among biblical scholars, have shaken the foundation upon which the preacher stands. Pointing to differences of opinion over the proposed ordination of homosexuals as an extreme example, Buttrick gives voice to the fundamental question that gives rise to contemporary doubts: "If interpreters can and on occasion do produce radically different readings of the same Scripture, where is authority? Is authority in texts, in interpretation, in methodology, or in some sort of theological pre-understanding on the part of scholars?"[9]

The answer to Buttrick's second question, of course, is yes. If the preacher's authority is grounded in the message of the biblical text, it also depends upon interpretation. A wrong interpretation forfeits the authority of the text. Interpretation, in turn, is affected by methodology. Not all hermeneutical methods are legitimate. Furthermore, the preacher's understanding of the text is inevitably shaped by the theological assumptions he or she brings to the text. But these lines of authority are not all equal. Nor are they in competition with one another. It is not as if the preacher's methods or assumptions can function on a separate trajectory, one that is independent from the text. There is an implied direction in the process of hermeneutics that radiates out from the biblical text. Eliminate the text and you eliminate the need for hermeneutics. This fact alone gives the text the place of primacy.

The crisis of confidence in modern preaching is also a result of the tendency to confuse authority with credibility. Though clearly related, these two are not identical. While there is an objective dimension to authority, credibility is a matter of perception. Authority can go unrecognized and yet still exist. Credibility, on the other hand, like beauty, rests in the eye of the beholder. When credibility becomes the only concern for preaching, the weight of authority for the sermon shifts from the text to the listener. The authority of the biblical text becomes subordinate to the preferences (and often the prejudices) of the listener. No one would argue that preachers should ignore the question of credibility. Yet it is worth noting how assiduously the apostle Paul avoided some things that would have earned him credibility in the eyes of his Corinthian hearers. In particular, the apostle avoided certain rhetorical elements that were especially valued by the Greeks (1 Cor. 2:1–4). As a result, his credibility suffered (2 Cor. 10:10). This made his preaching ministry more difficult but did not erode his authority.

The biblical text is the true location for the preacher's authority because it is the vehicle God uses to express himself and his will. God so identifies himself with the words of the Bible that he claims the words of the biblical authors as his own. Timothy Ward describes the relationship between God and his words as being ontological in nature. To encounter God's words is to encounter God, and to trust God's words is an act of trusting in God himself.[10] This was the case not only in those few instances in which God engaged in direct address but also of the recorded words of those who spoke on his behalf—the writers of Holy Scripture.

This relationship between God and the biblical text is reflected in the language of Scripture itself. B. B. Warfield points to two classes of biblical passages which together "make an irresistible impression of the absolute identification by the writers of the Scriptures in their hands with the living voice of God."[11] In one class, the Scriptures and God are so identified with one another that the Scriptures are sometimes spoken of as if they were God. In the other, God is spoken of as if he were the Scriptures.[12]

Is the Preacher Necessary?

If Timothy Ward is correct when he asserts that those who encounter God's Word encounter God, why not dispense with the preacher altogether? Maybe what the church really needs today is not preachers at all but readers.

The lector certainly has a place in worship. Paul considered the public reading of Scripture an important element in the church's teaching ministry (1 Tim. 4:13). Yet his command that Timothy devote himself to exhortation and instruction as well as to public reading is proof that more is needed than merely hearing the words of the biblical text. Of the three elements mentioned in 1 Timothy 4:13, the last two (preaching and teaching) require more than a reader. Preaching is necessary; the preacher is necessary.

The presence of the preacher implies the need for someone to do what the text alone does not do, at least not automatically. To say this may sound as if we are placing the preacher above the text.

This would be a mistake. <u>The proper location for those who preach</u> <u>is always under the text. The preacher's words share the authority of</u> <u>the text only to the extent that they agree with the text.</u> Scripture is <u>God's word.</u> The words of the sermon are the preacher's words about God's word. Scripture is the sole authority for faith and practice in the believer's life. But the authority and sufficiency of Scripture should not lead us to conclude that the power of God's Word works like a magic spell. The God who gave the Scriptures also gave the church preachers and teachers to help the church understand what is written (Rom. 12:7; 1 Cor. 12:28–29; Eph. 4:11–12).

John Stott observes that biblical exposition not only presupposes that Scripture is inspired; it assumes that the biblical text is to some degree closed. Such an assumption does not contradict the Reformation doctrine of the clarity of Scripture. "The Reformers' insistence on the perspicuity of Scripture referred to its central message, the gospel of salvation through faith in Christ crucified. That is as plain as day in the Bible," Stott asserts. "But the Reformers did not claim that everything in Scripture was equally plain. How could they, when Peter wrote that some things in Paul's letters were 'hard to understand' (2 Peter 3:15–16)?"[13] Preaching or exposition, then, involves more than simply restating the text. "To expound Scripture is to bring out of the text what is there and expose it to view," Stott explains. "The expositor prizes open what appears to be closed, makes plain what is obscure, unravels what is knotted and unfolds what is tightly packed."[14]

The Old Testament example of Ezra provides a biblical prototype for this task. Ezra is one of the Babylonian exiles who returned to Jerusalem during the reign of Artaxerxes and is described as "a teacher well versed in the Law of Moses" (Ezra 7:6). Assisted by the Levites, Ezra's practice was to read from the book of the law, "making it clear and giving the meaning so that the people could understand what was being read" (Neh. 8:8). Translation certainly was an important part of this process. The law was written in Hebrew, and the returning exiles spoke Aramaic. But translation is also interpretive work. Ezra and his companions laid the foundation for the scribes and rabbis of Jesus' day, who understood their responsibility to include not only the restatement of the law but its interpretation and application. While Jesus did not always agree with their conclusions, he did recognize the need for such work (Matt. 13:52). Like Ezra, preachers declare God's Word, explain its meaning, and draw out its implications for their listeners.

Those who preach speak for God. They carry on the conversation that was begun when God spoke the world into existence at creation. They echo the words spoken through the prophets "at many times and in various ways." But more than anything else, those who preach trumpet God's final word by preaching Christ crucified.

chapter 6

WORD
AND SERMON

Not long ago, after I had preached, a man came up and asked if he could talk with me. "I have a word from the Lord for you," he said. This isn't the kind of comment one usually likes to hear immediately following the sermon. After all, didn't Ehud the left-handed Benjamite say something similar to Eglon the fat king of Moab just before he thrust in the knife? It is the sort of thing people say just before they stick it to you.

The man who told me this had that distracted look we generally associate with prophets—and with those who mutter to themselves as they pass you on the street. I watched as he cocked his head and gazed off into the distance, like someone who turns the dial to the far end of the radio band and strains to hear the faint signal from a hard to reach station.

"The Lord wants you to be fully devoted to him," he said at last.

Who could argue with that? I could think of several areas in my life that left plenty of room for improvement. But what this would-be prophet said next took me by surprise.

After another pause, he said, "God wants you to stop using notes when you preach."

That was when I concluded that my new friend, though sincere and well meaning, was probably not speaking for God. Because it seemed to me that if God really did have such a message for me, he would have given me some inkling while I was preparing my sermon. Not a voice from heaven, necessarily, but at least some inner sense that what I was doing was wrong. More than anything else, I couldn't help marveling at his inference that my use of a manuscript, my planning nearly every word of the sermon in advance, somehow reflected a lack of devotion to God. From my point of view, the hours spent praying over and carefully crafting the language of the sermon signaled the opposite.

There are, of course, many good reasons for preaching without notes. You don't have the distraction of shuffling paper. The pulpit does not stand between the preacher and the listener. People like it when you look them in the eye. But the most compelling reason offered by proponents of preaching without notes is a spiritual one. They seem to share a common assumption that the Holy Spirit is more active in extemporaneous speech than he is in planned speech and that those who preach without notes are better able to sense the moving of the Holy Spirit.[1]

Why Language Matters

It is one thing to say that extemporaneous preaching is more suited to a certain context, personality type, or set of gifts. It is something quite different to contend that the use of a manuscript actually hinders the Holy Spirit. This is a curious assumption for those who also believe that the Scriptures — words committed to manuscript long ago — are the chief means that the Holy Spirit uses to speak to us today. When circumstances do not allow us to plan before we speak, we can trust the Holy Spirit to provide the necessary words (Matt. 10:19). But there are also good reasons for choosing our words in advance. One good reason is to do justice to the language of the sermon.

The language of the sermon matters because words matter to God. The Bible's voice is broadly inflected. It speaks to us in a variety of genres, styles, and vocabularies. This diversity is not an accident. As J. I. Packer puts it, "the Lord who gave the Word also gave the words."[2] The biblical doctrine of inspiration teaches that the Holy Spirit's influence extended to more than the ideas recorded in the Bible. This means that the words of the writers of Scripture were "breathed out" by God (2 Tim. 3:16). But they were also the writers' own words. The Holy Spirit did not blot out the authors' vocabulary or personal style as they were "carried along" in the process of inspiration (2 Peter 1:21).

B. B. Warfield explains, "One would suppose it to lie in the very nature of the case that if the Lord makes any revelation to men, He would do it in the language of men; or to individualize more explicitly, in the language of the man He employs as the organ of His revelation; and that naturally means, not the language of his nation or circle merely, but his own particular language, inclusive of all that gives individuality to his self-expression."[3] In inspiration, "God uses the instruments He employs in accordance with their natures."[4]

In the Scriptures, God uses the "particular language" of those who spoke and wrote on his behalf. John's grammatical style, for example, is simple, while Luke's writing is so polished that New Testament scholar F. F. Bruce called him an "artist in words."[5] Yet despite the simplicity of John's language, it is clear that he also chose his words carefully and with purpose. Kerry Inman cites the extensive analysis of John's writing made by Edwin A. Abbot, who demonstrated that the apostle's vocabulary, though small, combined theological purpose with artistry. Abbot concluded that John's use of language showed him to be "a master of words in the prime of his intellect."[6]

Paul too acknowledged the importance of language when he determined not to come to the Corinthians "with eloquence or superior wisdom" (1 Cor. 2:1). Far from suggesting that words are incidental to the message, the apostle's resolve bore witness to the power and importance of language. Words can obscure as well as reveal (1 Cor. 1:17). The same words that God uses to enlighten can be twisted by others to deceive (Eph. 5:6).

A Stewardship of Language

We exercise a kind of dominion with our words. Language is a realm where God has assigned us "a measure of independent power."[7] This is true of all speech, but it is especially true for the preacher. Like those who inscribed the words of Holy Scripture, the language we use in preaching is our "own particular language." We who speak for God have been granted the liberty to choose our own words. Barth was right to characterize the speech of preaching as "free" speech.[8]

Yet this freedom to frame the message in our own words is also a responsibility. Dominion implies stewardship. The most familiar dimension of this stewardship has to do with the content of our message. We have been granted freedom to choose our words, but not our gospel. Not even angels exercise that freedom (Gal. 1:8). To preach is to be bound to the gospel and the truths that arise from it. The preacher cannot say just anything. There are certain doctrines that the church is obliged to teach (Titus 2:1).

This stewardship is vividly pictured by Paul when he describes the church as "the pillar and foundation of the truth" (1 Tim. 3:15). We might have expected him to reverse the order, to say that the truth is the pillar and foundation of the church. In fact, he implies this very thing when he says that the church is built upon the "foundation of the apostles and prophets" (Eph. 2:20). Or to change the analogy and the geography slightly, the church is under the Word, not the other way around. The church is under the authority of Scripture and bound by what it commands. Yet there is a kind of reciprocal relationship between the church and the Word. The same church which is built upon the foundation of the Word and is answerable to the Word is also responsible for the Word. The Word of God is living and active

(Heb. 4:12). But it is also passive and vulnerable. The same word that has power to give life to those who are spiritually dead can languish by the wayside and be trampled underfoot by the profane (Luke 8:5). It can be diluted and sold for profit (2 Cor. 2:17).

The church also exercises a stewardship over the kind of language it uses to convey this message. The freedom we have to choose our words is not absolute freedom. One limiting factor is the particularity of the ideas contained in the text. The biblical writers meant to express specific ideas to a specific audience. One aim of preaching is to put these ideas on display. If we are to accomplish this, we must be as certain as possible that the words we use are fit words. The language we use must be suited to the ideas we are trying to express.

Leon Morris offers an example of this when he argues that *propitiation* is a better word for describing Christ's work than *expiation*. According to Morris, expiation is the inferior of the two because it describes an impersonal process by which the effects of sin are nullified. To speak of Christ's work as merely expiation does not take the wrath of God into account. Propitiation, on the other hand, speaks of a personal process. Morris observes, "When it comes to speaking about Christ's atoning work, it makes a great deal of difference which meaning we understand."[9]

Our words must also fit the context. The aptly spoken word of Proverbs 25:11 is a word that is suited to the circumstance. We have all had the awkward experience of listening to someone whose words were ill suited to the context. Perhaps they were too light in view of the gravity of the situation. Or maybe they spoke with sonorous importance when they should have told a joke. Thomas G. Long speaks of "the casual, chatty preachers of the relaxed suburban congregation, welcoming people with the perkiness of a TV weathercaster and running through the joys and concerns as if they were the recreational program directions of a cruise ship."[10] It is hard to imagine a sermon like Jonathan Edwards' "Sinners in the Hands of an Angry God" being preached by the kind of preachers Long describes. Their chief error is not the chatty style they employ, so much as it is the fact that their style is never otherwise. I have also heard preachers who seemed to think that every sermon was an occasion for pronouncing seven woes upon the congregation. Either way, the result is the same: an emotional monotone which flattens the affective dimension of the text. In addition to the particular ideas conveyed by the passage, each text has a particular tone that should shape our choice of words. There is "a time to weep and a time to laugh, a time to mourn and a time to dance" (Eccl. 3:4). Sometimes all in the same sermon.

Language and Culture

Fit words are also suited to the culture of the audience. Language is a basic component of human culture. The peculiar accent of one's native tongue is more than a collection of sounds arranged in distinct patterns; it is also a way of looking at the world and organizing ideas. Neil Postman observes that language has a hidden ideological agenda: "In the case of language, that agenda is so deeply integrated into our personalities and world-view that a special effort and, often, special training are required to detect its presence."[11] If this is true, then every word we utter is potentially an exercise in cross-cultural communication.

According to the Babel account in Genesis 11, a common tongue was one of the factors that unified rebellious humanity after the flood. God "confused" human language to divide and scatter the nations (Gen. 11:6–7). At Pentecost, this judgment underwent a unique reversal.[12] But instead of restoring a common tongue, those who came to Jerusalem from "every nation under heaven" heard the gospel proclaimed in their own language (Acts 2:5–6). This event set the pattern for all of the church's proclamation. Even when the audience's native language is the same as ours, preaching is always an exercise in translation. We are bound by the ideas of the biblical text when we preach, but we are also constrained by the culture and life situation of those who hear us. As we put the ideas of the biblical text on display, we draw out specific implications for a specific audience. If we are to fulfill our responsibility as God's messengers, we must deliver his message in language that our listeners can understand.

It is tempting to assign each of these forces its own pole in the sermon — to say, for example, that the text governs exegesis and hermeneutics while the audience controls specific application and the mode of proclamation. It is true that the biblical author and the life situation of the original audience dominate the exegetical and hermeneutical phases of the sermon. Yet even in these early stages, those who will be listening to us are never far from view. Our awareness of the audience during the exegetical process affects the angle of vision we take on the text, creating a kind of filter that determines which exegetical and hermeneutical data we will select for emphasis.

This is not the same as allowing the audience to take control of the text during exegesis. Meaning always originates with the author. But the audience has a voice in what aspects of the author's meaning should occupy our attention. Conversely, the biblical author has a say in the implications that can be drawn from the text. Our applications are influenced as much by the original context of the passage as they are by our audience's situation. We may draw conclusions from the text that its human author never envisioned, but we cannot make applications that are incompatible with the author's intent. Meaning originates with the author, and any legitimate application must be consistent with the text's meaning.

The explicit application of Leviticus 19:9, for example, is as concrete as it is clear: "When you reap the harvest of your land, do not reap to the very edges of your field or gather the gleanings of your harvest." However, such an application would be meaningless to most listeners today. Even in a congregation of farmers, literal adherence to this command would be unlikely to achieve its intended effect. The poor would not know to profit from the unharvested corners of the farmer's field. There is also a theological challenge when applying such a text. How do we preach such a passage to those who are not under the law of Moses? The specifics no longer apply, but its prinicple is still binding. Moses' command to make provision for the poor is mirrored in the New Testament (2 Cor. 8:7; 9:6–12; Gal. 2:10). This command might be fufilled in ways today that Moses could not have imagined.

Why We Should Weigh Our Words

The language of the sermon matters because not all words have the same value. Many words are common. They are like the vessels of wood or clay in an ancient house, frequently used and easily handled. The strength of such words is also their weakness. They are so familiar to those who hear them that they often go unnoticed. Other words are used more sparingly. They are kept in reserve like your grandmother's fragile china, only to be brought out when the nature of the moment or the content of the message requires a special dignity.

Unfortunately, we live in an age that no longer cares to weigh its words. As John McWhorter, professor of linguistics at the University of California at Berkley, notes, "America no longer values carefully wrought oral expression in the way that it did even in the recent past."[13] After comparing American political speeches of the mid-twentieth century with those of the nineteenth century, McWhorter concludes that the modern speech maker "tends to strongly operate under a guiding imperative not to sound too high a note."[14] Because spoken language is preferred over written, American public address is marked by contractions, slang, and short economical sentences that aim more for emotional impact than for cognitive reflection. Indeed, McWhorter could be describing many contemporary sermons when he characterizes modern speeches as "mostly symbolic exercises packaging a few large points in short, punchy sentences" whose "goal is the gut rather than the head."[15]

The preference for this kind of language goes beyond the aesthetic. McWhorter points to the moral importance attributed to casual speech when he observes that modern America has become a country "where rigorously polished language, of a sort only possible when channeled through the deliberate activity of writing, is considered insincere."[16]

However, in the sermon, carefully chosen words put a face on the text and bring the ideas of the passage to life. It is a mistake to view the preacher's words as merely incidental to the sermon. The ideas of the sermon cannot be separated from the words we use to express them. My colleague Rosalie de Rosset is correct when she observes, "Language is not, after all, so much the dress of thought as the incarnation of thought. The Word is truth become flesh. Language is the body of the idea, and it is only in the body that we become aware of it."[17]

George Orwell believed there is a relationship between the quality of one's ideas and the quality of the language used to express them. Poor thinking leads to poor language, which in turn fosters even poorer thinking. Our language "becomes ugly and inaccurate because our thoughts are foolish, but the slovenliness of our language makes it easier for us to have foolish thought."[18]

In addition to its stale imagery, lack of precision, and stock phrases, slovenly language is mechanical. When the public speaker resorts to it, "the appropriate noises are coming out of his larynx, but his brain is not involved as it would be if he were choosing his words for himself. If the speech he is making is one that he is accustomed to make over and over again, he may be almost unconscious of what he is saying, as one is when one utters the responses in church."[19]

The confessional nature of evangelical preaching makes it especially vulnerable to this sort of empty repetition. But repetition and familiarity do not inevitably lead to boredom. Augustine pointed out that well written words can be received with delight not only by those who first read them but also by those who reread them.[20] Many of us have had this experience when returning to the worn pages of a favorite book or upon hearing a beloved song when it is played again. Augustine agreed with Cicero that the experience of delight is one of the three marks of true eloquence. One who is eloquent should speak in a way that teaches, delights, and moves.[21] Teaching, as Augustine defines it, is a function of our doctrine. It depends upon what we have to say. But delight and persuasion are functions of our language. Whether our hearers are delighted and moved depends upon the way we say what we have to say.

A Shared Responsibility

It should be added that we are not the only responsible parties in this transaction. Listening, like reading, requires focused attention, and not everyone is willing to pay the price. C. S. Lewis warns that there is a kind of reader who actually prefers clichés. For such a person, it is the emblematic nature of the cliché that makes it so appealing. Lewis offers the cliché "my blood ran cold" as an example, explaining that it serves as a hieroglyph for fear. "Any attempt, such as a great writer might make, to render *this* fear in its full particularity, is doubly a chokespear to the unliterary reader," Lewis warns. "For it offers him what he doesn't want, and offers it only on condition of his giving to the words a kind and degree of attention that he does not intend to give. It is like trying to sell him something he has no use for at a price he does not wish to pay."[22]

What is true of the unliterary reader is also true of those who hear our sermons. For some, the tedium of the cliché and the formulaic statement are actually a comfort. Not because they provide an anchor to the church's foundational truths but because they create the illusion of listening without any actual hearing taking place. The cliché is preferred because it is undemanding. It requires no effort. Because the cliché substitutes mere apprehension for comprehension, it allows listeners to maintain emotional distance. Instead of putting flesh on the truth and making it concrete in all its particularity, the cliché presents a one-dimensional icon in its place.

Here, then, is another reason to be intentional about the language we use in preaching. We frame the message in intentional and well crafted language in the hope that it will help reluctant listeners focus their attention. Words are the lens we use to close the distance between the audience and the sermon and to make the ideas of the sermon concrete. If our words do not arouse them from their slumber like a lover's kiss, then perhaps they will be strong enough to arrest attention and compel them to look more closely at the truth that has been put on display.

No wonder a sermon like "Sinners in the Hands of an Angry God" made the people of Enfield grip the pews and shriek in terror. Surely the occasion was not the first time those descendants of the Puritans had ever heard a sermon about hell. But Edwards had crafted the language of this particular sermon to make those who were already familiar with the church's teaching on this subject "sensible" of this truth. If hell is real, Edwards explained, then "he does me the best kindness, that does most to represent to me the truth of the case, that sets forth my misery and dangers in the liveliest manner."[23]

Words that are chosen merely for the sake of ornament are a gaudy distraction in the sermon. Carefully chosen words, like a well crafted necklace, accent the true shape of the ideas expressed in Scripture. But unlike the string of pearls that adorns a woman's neck yet is distinct from it, words cannot be separated from the ideas they express.

Do extemporaneous words have more power than words committed to paper? The answer depends as much upon the nature of words themselves as it does upon the ideas they represent. The Holy Spirit can speak as powerfully through a sermon delivered with the help of a manuscript as he can through one delivered extemporaneously. Scripture itself is proof of the Holy Spirit's ability to use a manuscript. If extemporaneous preaching has the advantage of immediacy, the use of a manuscript enables the preacher to think carefully about what kind of words are best suited to the message. Whatever the mode of expression, they must be words that are worthy. Vessels fit enough to convey the ideas of the sermon, and able to be received by those who hear.

chapter 7

PROPHET, PRIEST, OR STAND-UP COMEDIAN?

The first sermon I can remember hearing was preached by a pastor whose thundering declamation seemed to rattle the light fixtures. I was in elementary school at the time. I do not remember a word of his message, only the terror it inspired in me. Perhaps that is why I recoiled at my mother's beaming delight when she learned that I felt called to preach.

"Oh, Johnny," she gushed, "you'd make a darling minister."

Darling was not the kind of preaching I had in mind. I did not want to mouth poetry in a clergyman's tame frock. I had no intention of becoming a "darling minister." Camel's hair and thundering declamation were more my style. I aspired to the prophet's mantle.

Preaching in the Marketplace

The kind of preachers we become depends to a great extent upon our mental image of what a preacher is. According to Thomas G. Long, "preachers have at least tacit images of the preacher's role, primary metaphors that not only describe the nature of the preacher but also embrace by implication all the other crucial aspects of the preaching event."[1] This inner vision is often an imprint left by the force of personal experience. Our idea of what it means to preach is a mirror of those we have heard (or perhaps read) and admire. Our listeners are not the only ones who follow Paul or Apollos because of their style. We are just as prone to identify ourselves by and shape our ministries after our heroes.

But our expectations of ourselves are also influenced by the expectations our listeners have of us. In Athens, Paul took his stand in the marketplace and challenged the ideas of the philosophers (Acts 17:17 – 18). Today the marketplace is not merely a location. It is a way of thinking. Those who are seated before us see themselves as an audience, a self-identity that has been shaped primarily by the culture of television. This is a realm where ideas really are on the market and credence is given based on the quality of a viewer's experience. As a result, the church has opinions about how it wishes to be addressed that are as strong — perhaps even stronger — than its notions of what it wants to hear. Today's listeners are more conscious of a speaker's image than they are of a sermon's line of reasoning, strength of argument, or its biblical content. We who preach to them have also been steeped in this culture and are tempted to try to hold their attention by the power of personality alone.

Since television is used to sell everything from deodorant to funerals, it is not surprising that some have urged contemporary preachers to look to this medium for role models in communicating the gospel.[2] However, the ethos of television is radically opposed to the prophetic ethos of preaching. A quarter of a century ago, when television evangelists like Jim Bakker, Jimmy Swaggart, and Jerry Falwell were in their prime, Neil Postman warned that there are "several characteristics of television and its surround that converge to make authentic religious experience impossible."[3]

But it is television's marketplace culture that is most hostile to preaching. James Twitchell observes, "The purpose of television is to keep you watching television, at least long enough to see the advertisements. Choice is the tribute the medium pays to the attention span."[4] From its Nielsen ratings, which enable broadcasters to gauge the level of viewer interest, to its seemingly infinite menu of program choices that can be recorded and watched whenever one pleases, television gives the (mostly false) impression that the viewer is in control of the experience. The prophet's message has the opposite effect. It reminds us that God is in control and we are accountable to him. The prophet does not try to make us feel comfortable or worry about whether we have enjoyed the experience. His chief concern is to arrest our attention and speak the truth (1 Kings 22:14, 16).

The prophetic model is an improvement over that of the television personality, but it is not the only biblical image which shapes our understanding of what it means to be a preacher. There is also a priestly dimension to the ministry of God's Word. The apostle Paul acknowledges this when he describes the proclamation of the gospel as a "priestly duty" (Rom. 15:16). It is tempting to see our own work in this language. We have spent hours in prayer and study, doing our best to make certain that the sermon will be acceptable in God's sight. We place ourselves at God's disposal when we stand before God's people to deliver the message. Our preaching is both an offering and an act of worship. This is how John Chrysostom characterized his ministry of preaching, describing it as "a great and august sacrifice, better than all others."[5]

Priestly Advocacy

Priests, like prophets, exercised a ministry of God's Word (Lev. 10:11). The priest, however, differed from the prophet because he shouldered an additional burden, serving as the people's advocate. Priests were not only "selected from among men" but were "appointed to represent them" (Heb. 5:1). Like the priest, the preacher does not stand apart from those who hear but is called from among them in order to sympathize with them (Heb. 4:15). Whenever we take our place before God's people to declare his Word, we also take upon ourselves this responsibility of advocacy. We may stand above or before the congregation in order to be seen or for the sake of acoustics, but our true location is in their midst. We speak to the people, but we are also for them.

The key to priestly advocacy is identification (Heb. 2:17). This means that the preacher functions as a kind of mediator, standing between the text and the congregation and listening to the Word of God on their behalf. Because we stand in their place, we ask the questions our listeners would ask. Some of these questions are obvious. Many are mundane. But if we are to be true advocates, we must also ask the questions our listeners would like to ask but dare not.

This, more than anything else, is what differentiates the priestly element of preaching from the prophetic. The prophetic nature of preaching gives us authority to make demands of the listener. The priestly nature of preaching obligates us to make demands of the text. It compels us to take our cue from the patriarchs, the psalms, and the apostles, as well as from the prophets, and ask God to justify himself: Will not the judge of the earth do right? How long, O Lord? Why have you afflicted us?

We give voice to the silent questions that plague our listeners, but we do not necessarily answer them. Our priestly role demands that we speak the truth, and the truth is: God does not always explain himself. Part of the priestly responsibility of preaching is to give voice to the congregation's unspoken questions and then listen with them to the awkward silence that sometimes ensues once the words have been spoken.

It is not our job to answer all of the congregation's questions. As Frederick Buechner observed, there is great pressure placed upon us, not only from the congregation but from within ourselves, to supply an answer: "The answer is what people have come to hear and what he has also come to hear, preaching always as much to himself as to anybody, to keep his spirits up."[6] Buechner rightly labels such efforts public relations rather than preaching. We aim for a higher goal.

Priestly advocacy should not be confused with trite slogans, pat answers, or simplistic explanations. Unfortunately, our culture's bent toward pragmatism makes us especially vulnerable in this area. We are too eager to come to God's defense, too quick to fill in the silences God leaves behind and attempt to explain what he himself has not explained.

Because we want to send our hearers away with something "practical," we are tempted to resort to lists, truisms, and oversimplification. In a misguided effort to compensate for God's silent presence, we offer conventional wisdom that has been dressed up in Sunday clothes and brought to church. Often what we introduce as "the thing the biblical writer is trying to say" isn't necessarily biblical or even distinctively Christian. At best, it is a reflection of common grace, an example of the homespun wisdom that God grants to all of humanity. Thomas G. Long warns, "Sermons on 'Five Ways to Keep Your Marriage Alive' or 'Keys to a Successful Prayer Life' or even 'Standing Up for Peace in a Warring World' may possess some ethical wisdom and some utilitarian helpfulness, but they often have the sickly sweet aroma of smoldering incense in a temple from which the deity has long since departed. They can easily have the sound of the lonely wisdom of Job's friends, who can quote the Psalms and the Proverbs but have ceased to expect the whirlwind."[7]

But then, what other kind of preaching would we expect from a church that has taken its cues from the marketplace? Why should we be surprised when our prophets learn at the feet of Madison Avenue pitchmen and our priests aspire to be television talk-show hosts?

Preaching the Rough Edges

Priestly advocacy means that we will not be afraid to faithfully portray the rough edges of the biblical text. The world in which the text was given was a world like our own, a world whose heroes were

more likely to be thugs than theologians. This was a world popu-
lated by people with troubled marriages and rebellious children. These
were men and women who found it hard to take God at his word
and seemed to have a gift for making the wrong choice. People who
laughed and wept and sometimes got mad enough to kill. People "just
like us" (James 5:17). You would hardly guess it from listening to our
sermons, in which many of the inconsistencies and ambiguities of
their character have been smoothed away. In such sermons, Samson's
sensuality, narcissism, and clumsy wit disappear, along with Gideon's
cowardice and doubt. We are not shocked by Abraham's eagerness to
put his wife's virtue in jeopardy for the sake of personal gain, nor are
we comforted by the dull faith and persistent failure of the apostles.
And we are hardly moved at all by the weeping of Christ.

One reason is because we have idealized the text. The contours
of the story remain, but the characters have become two dimensional.
We tame the text through selective observation, careless reading, and
sometimes outright rehabilitation. The result is as flat and cartoonlike
as the flannelgraph pictures our Sunday school teachers used when
they taught them to us as children. This may be conducive for transforming the rough and blemished characters who inhabit these biblical stories into moral examples. But it does not work well as a mirror.
We cannot see ourselves in such texts.

The other damaging effect of this flattening is its tendency to
normalize the outrageous in Scripture. We treat these stories as if the
events they describe are business as usual, thus stealing the wonder
from the text and making it impossible for us to grasp the reckless
extravagance of God's grace. But to those who first experienced them,
God's way of dealing with sinners must have seemed exceedingly
strange. The God who makes the rules does not play by them. The
race does not go to the swift. Favor is not granted to the deserving.

These biblical accounts are teeming with dubious heroes and
undeserved reversals of fortune. Cain and Jonah, the prodigal son's
elder brother, and Simon Peter all share the same indignation and ask

the same question. The chorus that rises from the pages of the Bible is a common one: Lord, what could you possibly have been thinking? Yet it is the question that is missing from many sermons. It is the question that reveals to us the true aim of these biblical accounts: not to make us comfortable but to astonish and at times dismay us.

All of which points to the real reason we have trouble seeing ourselves in these stories. It is because we have also misread the text of our own lives. We idealize the biblical text because we have idealized our own experience. We want to live in a world that is governed by formulas and rules. We want to believe that there really are five ways to keep your marriage alive or three keys to a healthy prayer life. Life, unfortunately, does not appear to be aware of the rules. "Nature seems to catch you by the tail," Annie Dillard observes. "I think of all the butterflies I have seen whose torn hind wings bore the jagged marks of bird's bills."[8] The same could be said of life. God's people file into place every Sunday, similarly scarred by the jagged marks left over from the previous week. They greet one another politely and turn their attention to us, quietly wondering why the rules did not apply to them and the formula did not work.

"I am a frayed and nibbled survivor in a fallen world, and I am getting along," Dillard writes. "I am aging and eaten and have done my share of eating too. I am not washed and beautiful, in control of a shining world in which everything fits, but instead am wandering awed about on a splintered wreck I've come to care for, whose gnawed trees breathe delicate air, whose bloodied and scarred creatures are my dearest companions, and whose beauty shines not *in* its imperfections but overwhelmingly in spite of them, under the wind-rent clouds, upstream and down."[9] She is writing about the natural world, but she could be describing the church.

A Failure of Imagination

In the film *Cool Hand Luke*, Strother Martin's character says to Paul Newman's character, "What we've got here is a failure to communicate." Martin's character complains further that there are some men that you just can't reach. We are inclined to agree with him. But when it comes to our preaching, the failure is as liable to be one of imagination as it is to be one of communication. What we've got here is a lack of imagination.

For nearly a century now, the evangelical pulpit has labored under the assumption that the root problem for preachers is a failure to communicate and that the key to communication is realism. This is a quality we try to instill in our sermons by giving attention to the historical details of the text, supporting our assertions with facts and figures, and using contemporary illustrations to assure our audience that the Bible is still "relevant." This desire to preach realistically has produced in us an obsession with pragmatism. We are so consumed with realism that we have forgotten to use our imagination. And imagination, it turns out, is the secret to realism in preaching.

Northrop Frye explains how this is so by drawing a distinction between the imaginary, which is unreal, and the imaginative, which gives shape and language to what is universal. The realm of the imaginative, Frye explains, is the realm of the poet: "The poet's job is not to tell you what happened, but what happens: not what did take place, but the kind of thing that always does take place. He gives you the typical, recurring, or what Aristotle calls universal event."[10] This is one of the primary functions of literature—to provide us with a typology by which we may recognize ourselves. "You wouldn't go to Macbeth to learn about the history of Scotland—you go to it to learn what a man feels like after he's gained a kingdom and lost his soul," Frye explains. "When you meet such a character as Micawber in Dickens, you don't feel that there must have been a man Dickens knew who was exactly like this: you feel that there's a bit of Micawber in almost everybody you know, including yourself."[11]

The imagination exercises an even greater power by enabling us not only to apprehend with our intellect what would otherwise be abstract but to experience it in some measure. According to C. S. Lewis, this is the value of myth. This sort of understanding is a matter of tasting rather than knowing, an experience of truth that transcends truth: "What flows into you from the myth is not truth but reality (truth is always *about* something, but reality is *about which* truth is), and, therefore, every myth becomes the father of innumerable truths on an abstract level."[12]

Lewis's assertion that in Christ "myth became fact" may make us uncomfortable. But he does not mean the same thing by this that Rudolf Bultmann does when he argues that the New Testament view of the world is "essentially mythical in character" and that to expect modern man to accept it would be "both senseless and impossible."[13] Lewis does not deny the historicity of the incarnation, death, and resurrection of Christ: "The heart of Christianity is a myth which is also a fact. The old myth of the Dying God, *without ceasing to be myth*, comes down from the heaven of legend and imagination to the earth of history. It *happens*—at a particular date, in a particular place, followed by definable historical consequences."[14]

When Lewis describes these historical events as myth, he is pointing to their capacity to engage the imagination in a way that enables us to experience the reality about which the gospel truth speaks. It is the gospel's mythic nature that guarantees its realism, and the imagination is the sphere in which this encounter takes place.

This explains why the Bible so often feels both familiar and alien at the same time. The people of the Bible are like us, and yet they are not. We share their fears and their failings. We identify with stories whose problems are like our own but whose particular details are unlike our experience. We recognize Moses' ambivalence, even though God has never spoken to us from a burning bush. We have not tried to walk on water, but we know what it is like to flounder. It is the mythic quality of their experience that makes them so recognizable.

Accessing the Imagination

If imagination is the vehicle by which we understand and apprehend the reality of biblical truth, how do we activate its power? In preaching, it is language that is the instrument—embodied both in the words of Scripture and our own words—which God uses to stimulate the imagination. Much has been said about the importance of visual images in today's culture. But it is language that is the primary gateway to the imagination. It is possible to tell a story by images alone. There may be instances in which a single picture is worth a thousand words. But there are things which language can do that no picture is capable of doing.

As J. R. R. Tolkien observes in his essay "On Fairy-Stories," the faculty of vision enables us to see the green grass and appreciate its beauty. The capacity of the human mind for generalization and abstraction allow us to distinguish the green grass from other things and see that it is green as well as grass. Through language, "We may put a deadly green upon a man's face and produce a horror; we may make the rare and terrible blue moon to shine; or we may cause woods to spring with silver leaves and rams to wear fleeces of gold, and put hot fire into the belly of the cold worm."[15]

It is just this hidden sense that we seek to stir when we speak to the imagination in preaching. When we do, we are not pressing into service something that is alien to the nature of God's Word. Neither are we appealing to the lower nature of our audience. According to nineteenth-century Scottish preacher John Ker, "The tokens of man's highest nature lie not in his being able to comprehend, but in his ability to feel that there are things which he cannot comprehend, and which he yet feels to be true and real, before which he is compelled to fall down in reverent awe."[16] Indeed, Ker warns that it is dangerous to deny or ignore the heart's need for this sense of wonder. When this happens, the heart takes revenge, seeking its nourishment "either in trifles or in morbid and unnatural shapes."[17]

According to Ker, our need for the experience of awe is manifested in three ways. First, by a craving for the new and fresh. God himself is unchanging, but his creation is marked by constant change. God has created us to be explorers. "Man's mind cannot long remain in a state of monotony without something like pain," Ker warns, "or, if it does, it is a sign of the low level to which the mind has sunk."[18]

Our need for awe is also ignited by a sense of beauty and grandeur. This is a higher order of appreciation than the love of the new, because it leads us from wonder to admiration. But it is the third dimension, in which we experience what Ker calls "wonder," that is most important. When we experience wonder, we move from admiration to awe. How does this happen? According to Ker, "It comes from the sense of what we can touch with our thought but cannot comprehend."[19]

This is our aim in preaching. To follow in the steps of the prophets and declare God's Word. To take our place in the midst of the people, standing between the text and the congregation and speaking as their advocate. But more than anything else, it is to provide those who hear us with a different kind of vision. To move our hearers to wonder. To enable them to touch with their thought things which they cannot comprehend. We speak with authority when we preach, but we also speak with sympathy. We declare certainties when we preach, but we also preside over mysteries. Preaching seeks to mediate the presence of Christ. By our words, we hope to kindle a flame on the altar of the heart.

chapter 8

PREACHING
AS GOSPEL

We are not the first to preach. We preach "the faith that was once for all entrusted to the saints" (Jude 1:3). This means that we take our cues from those who have preceded us. The church is built upon the foundation of the apostles and prophets, and Jesus came preaching before the apostles ever uttered a word of the gospel. Yet it takes only a cursory reading of the Gospels and Acts to sense that the preaching we engage in week by week sounds very different from theirs. How do we explain this?

To some extent it must be attributed to a difference in mission. Jesus came to do more than proclaim the gospel. He came to accomplish it. Jesus' central role in redemptive events and his location on the timeline of their fulfillment placed constraints on his preaching that we do not share. The result was an element of secrecy in Jesus' preaching. This intentional obscurity, which simultaneously revealed and concealed Christ's identity and his mission, is best exemplified by the parables of Christ.

Jesus was not the first to use parables. Some of the Old Testament prophets also employed parables in their preaching (Ezek. 17:2; 20:49; 24:3; Hos. 12:10). Yet New Testament scholar Joachim Jeremias observes, "We find nothing to be compared with the parables of Jesus, whether in the entire intertestamental literature of Judaism, the Essene writings, in Paul, or in Rabbinic literature."[1] The parables of Jesus were disarmingly familiar: "Their nearness to life, their simplicity and clarity, the masterly brevity with which they are told, the seriousness of their appeal to the conscience, their loving understanding of the outcasts of religion—all this is without analogy."[2]

Despite this incorporation of commonplace themes and familiar images, there is an opaque quality to Jesus' parables which hides the very thing they are intended to reveal. The meaning of many of his parables was not immediately apparent to Christ's disciples (Matt. 13:36; 15:15). When asked why he spoke to the crowd in parables, Jesus replied, "The knowledge of the secrets of the kingdom of heaven has been given to you, but not to them" (Matt. 13:11).

By employing parables, Jesus managed to be elusive and confrontational at the same time. Their very indirectness drew attention to Jesus. Jesus' parables piqued the interest of those who heard them and made it difficult to turn away, creating a decision point for those who heard. Howard Marshall explains, "By his method of teaching in parables Jesus not only invited his audiences to penetrate below the surface and find the real meaning; at the same time he allowed them the opportunity—which many of them took—of turning a blind eye and a deaf ear to the real point at issue."[3] For Jesus, then, parables were more than a communication technique. They served as a kind of litmus test which revealed those who had "ears to hear" (Mark 4:9, 23; Luke 8:8; 14:35).

Another unique feature of Jesus' preaching was its emphasis on the kingdom of God. We preach Christ, but Christ proclaimed the kingdom. Jeremias calls the kingly reign of God "the central theme of the public proclamation of Jesus."[4] Like the parables, Jesus' proc-

lamation of the kingdom shone a spotlight on his true identity and
mission by diverting attention away from himself. This has prompted
William Brosend to describe Jesus as "a Galilean Jew who proclaimed
a kingdom and resisted a crown."[5] According to Brosend, "Jesus is
consistently and persistently depicted as focusing the attention on God
and God's kingdom, not on himself."[6]

Brosend may be overstating the point somewhat. Jesus did speak
about himself during his ministry (Matt. 5:11; 10:22, 37–38; 11:6;
24:9; Mark 8:38; 13:9; 13:13; Luke 7:23; 9:26; 21:17). He asked what
others thought about him and was especially concerned that his disciples should understand who he was (Matt. 16:13–16; Mark 8:27–29;
Luke 9:18–20). His repeated warnings that the disciples would be
persecuted because of him implied a fundamental connection between
Jesus and apostolic preaching in the future. Yet the importance of the
kingdom to Jesus' message cannot be denied (Matt. 24:14). The kingdom is central in Mark's synopsis of Jesus' early ministry: "After John
was put in prison, Jesus went into Galilee, proclaiming the good news
of God. 'The time has come,' he said. 'The kingdom of God is near.
Repent and believe the good news!'" (Mark 1:14–15). In a corrobo-
ration of Mark's summation, Matthew says, "Jesus went throughout
Galilee, teaching in their synagogues, preaching the good news of the
kingdom, and healing every disease and sickness among the people"
(Matt. 4:23). Luke tells us that Jesus "proclaimed the good news of
the kingdom of God" and that he sent the Twelve out to "preach the
kingdom of God and to heal the sick" (Luke 8:1; 9:2).

The miracles of healing mentioned in these verses were also part
of this kingdom message. They were not exercises in pre-evangelism or
relief work in the way that social action and the healing arts are often
used by missionaries and churches today, but signs of divine power
and authority which served as proof of the nearness of the kingdom.
Even John (though to a lesser extent than Matthew, Mark, and Luke)
portrays a Christ who spoke of the kingdom (John 3:3, 5; 18:36).

Neither can it be denied that Jesus was often indirect when

referring to himself. Jesus' rhetorical strategy, according to Brosend, was "only occasionally self-referential."[7] Pointing to Mark 10:17 as an example, Brosend notes, "Neither here nor elsewhere in the Synoptics when Jesus is asked, 'What should I do to inherit eternal life?' does he say, 'Believe in me.'"[8] The gospel of John, of course, is a different story, something which Brosend acknowledges but does not discuss in detail.[9]

Apostolic Preaching

Jesus' reserve in speaking directly about himself in the Gospels was noted by Thomas Dehany Bernard in his 1864 series of Bampton Lectures on the "Progress of Doctrine in the New Testament." According to Bernard, this reserve was shared by the apostles during the early stages of their ministry, when they were sent out to announce the kingdom but forbidden to tell anyone that Jesus was the Christ (Matt. 16:20; 17:9). However, a marked change takes place in apostolic preaching in the book of Acts. The essential difference is captured in the summary statement of Acts 5:42: "Day after day, in the temple courts and from house to house, they never stopped teaching and proclaiming the good news that Jesus is the Christ." Here the announcement of the kingdom so prominent in the Gospels has given way to the explicit proclamation of Christ. "No such announcements as these are heard in the Gospels," Bernard explains. "The preaching spoken of there is not of the person but of the kingdom."[10]

This does not mean that the theme of the kingdom disappeared from the apostles' preaching after the resurrection.[11] Indeed, Acts opens and closes with an emphasis on teaching about the kingdom. At the beginning of the book, Jesus appears to the disciples over a period of forty days, offering convincing proofs of his resurrection and speaking about the kingdom of God (Acts 1:3). At the conclusion of Acts, Paul is in Rome proclaiming the kingdom "boldly and without hindrance" (Acts 28:31; cf. v. 23). These bookend statements help us to understand the exchange between Jesus and the disciples' in Acts

1:6–8. After listening to Jesus teach about the kingdom for forty days, the disciples understandably wanted to know whether the time had come to restore the kingdom to Israel. Jesus answered that the timing was none of their business. Instead, they were to bear witness to him: "But you will receive power when the Holy Spirit comes on you; and you will be my witnesses in Jerusalem, and in all Judea and Samaria, and to the ends of the earth" (Acts 1:8).

Consequently, in Acts the apostles continued to preach the gospel of the kingdom, but in the more particular terms of the person and work of Jesus Christ. As proof of this, Bernard points to Luke's concluding synopsis of Paul's teaching at Rome, which combined testimony about the kingdom with the proclamation of Christ: "Evidently on purpose are the two expressions combined in this final summary, in order to show that the preaching of the kingdom and the preaching of Christ are one: that the original proclamation has not ceased, but that in Christ Jesus the thing proclaimed is no longer a vague and future hope, but a distinct and present fact."[12]

This change in the content of the apostles' message was matched by a change in the effect of their preaching. Within a matter of days, the number of those who believed grew from hundreds to thousands (Acts 2:41; cf. Acts 6:7). Bernard attributed this to the apostles' proclamation of the nature and the spiritual consequences of Jesus' messiahship, noting that if the apostles had preached merely about Jesus' holy character, his moral beauty, or his winsome nature, the opposite would have taken place: "Then Jesus Christ ought to have gathered the thousands and his disciples the hundreds; and the faith inspired in the first period ought to have been more decided and intense than that awakened in the second."[13] It is not merely the shadow of the cross which separates these two periods of proclamation, but the reality of its power.

There is no more eloquent testimony to this in the New Testament than the example of the apostle Paul, who described the message he preached variously as "the word of faith," "the message of the cross," "the message of reconciliation," "the mystery of Christ," the "word of truth" and most commonly as "the gospel."[14] Paul trumpets his confidence in his message by declaring, "I am not ashamed of the gospel, because it is the power of God for the salvation of everyone who believes: first for the Jew, then for the Gentile" (Rom. 1:16).

Paul often employs a confessional tone when he summarizes his message in Scripture. The apostle's gospel involved the repetition of key themes, namely the suffering, death, and resurrection of Jesus Christ. He uses the common vocabulary of tradition, describing his message as something which he "received" and "passed on" to others (1 Cor. 15:3, cf. 11:2, 23; Matt. 15:3). For him all the music of the gospel ultimately resolved itself into a single note: "Jesus Christ and him crucified" (1 Cor. 2:2). This, Paul believed, should be the standard for the entire church (Gal. 1:6–9; 2:5; cf. 2 Cor. 11:4). What is clear from all of Paul's writings is that Christ is at the center of his theology and the cross is the anchor which holds its application in place. For Paul, all preaching was gospel preaching.

The Marginal Gospel

The same cannot be said for us. We have not abandoned the gospel. But we have relegated its message to the outskirts of our Christian experience. As a result, the gospel has been marginalized, reserved primarily for those who are on the threshold of faith. The gospel is now widely viewed as one of the "elementary truths" that we expect believers to "leave" when they are ready to "go on to maturity" (Heb. 6:1). We do not want them to forsake the gospel. But we do expect them to move on to other more important matters.

This is a conviction shared by our more mature listeners, whose hearts sink as soon as they suspect that the sermon is "just a gospel message." The gospel is something they have already heard. While they believe and appreciate it, they want to learn more about the God who gave the gospel. They do not want to be like those the writer of Hebrews complains about, who should have been teachers but needed someone to teach them the elementary truths of God's Word all over again (Heb. 5:12).

These assumptions, while understandable, are problematic. It is true that there is more to God's Word than the gospel, both theologically and practically. The horizon of subjects upon which the Bible touches is as wide as the scope of human experience. It addresses all the theological categories from theology proper to eschatology, and its concerns span the entire spectrum of ordinary life. But if our goal in preaching is for people to know God, it must be asked whether this is possible in any meaningful way apart from the gospel.

Our knowledge of God is dependent upon divine self-revelation. We would not know anything about God if he had not taken the initiative to reveal himself. This revelation has reached its apex in the person of Jesus Christ. It is true that it is possible to know things *about* God apart from Christ. The heavens declare the glory of God. Our consciences reveal his eternal power and divine nature (Ps. 19:1; Rom. 1:19–20). But this side of the incarnation, it is not possible to know God *relationally* except through Christ. This thought is implicit in Jesus' challenge to the Pharisees in John 8:19: "If you knew me, you would know my Father also." It is explicit in the assertion of Hebrews 1:1–2 that the God who in the past spoke to our forefathers through the prophets at many times and in various ways has in these last days spoken to us through his Son. Jesus is God's final and best word about himself. All that we know about God must be seen and understood through the lens which Christ provides.

Thomas F. Torrance notes, "In the language of the New Testament, preaching Christ involves *kerygma* and *didache*—it is both a kerygmatic and a didactic activity. It is both evangelical and theological."[15] The church's mistake, according to Torrance, has been to separate these two. One way this has been done is by separating the Christ of theology from the Christ of history. Torrance labels the Christ of history shorn of theological truth "an abstraction invented by pseudo-scientific method" and warns, "The historical Jesus and the theological Christ cannot be separated from one another without grave misunderstanding of the gospel and serious detriment to the faith of the church."[16] Separating the theological Christ from the Christ of history severs the church's theology from its mooring in the incarnation and removes any hope of knowing God as he intended us to know him. There is, as Torrance puts it, "no unknown God behind the back of Jesus for us to fear; to see the Lord Jesus is to see the very face of God."[17]

Another way the church has separated *kerygma* and *didache* is by detaching the application of our Christian faith from the gospel. It is easy to understand why some might want to relegate the gospel to the beginning of the Christian life. Coming to faith is one thing. Living out the reality of that faith is something else. Our listeners' disappointment when they hear a sermon that is "only the gospel" usually springs from the false assumption that the gospel has a single application. It unites us to Christ but has nothing to say about how we live for Christ. If, as Torrance says, it is damaging to the faith of the church to separate *kerygma* and *didache* evangelism, it is equally damaging to the preaching of the church for sermon applications to be detached from the theology of the cross.

The vital connection between the cross and Christian practice is expressed by Paul in Galatians 2:20: "I have been crucified with Christ and I no longer live, but Christ lives in me. The life I live in the body, I live by faith in the Son of God, who loved me and gave himself for me." Paul understood the Christian's daily life to be a cruciformed life, one in which the reality of our union with Christ in his death is reflected in ordinary practice. The Christian's daily life is also a resurrected life. This too is implicit in the message of the cross: "If we have been united with him like this in his death, we will certainly also be united with him in his resurrection" (Rom. 6:5). The message of the cross is incomplete without a corresponding proclamation of resurrection that spells out its implications for Christian practice. This is the apostolic pattern according to Richard Lischer: "The proclamation of

Christ's death and resurrection is always followed by an authoritative 'Therefore' (as in Romans 5:1), which connects the salvation event with the stories of our lives."[18]

This means that the gospel is for the believer as much as it is for the unbeliever. To marginalize the gospel by relegating it to the entry point of our faith and to ignore its application to the believer's daily experience is spiritually deadly. Torrance marvels that evangelicals often link the substitution of Christ with his death but not with his incarnate person and life. He believes that this undermines the radical nature of Christ's substitutionary work: "Substitution understood in this radical way means that Christ takes our place in all our human life and activity before God even in our believing, praying, and worshipping of God, for he has yoked himself to us in such a profound way that he stands in for us and upholds us at every point in our human relations before God."[19]

The gospel offers hope for the present life as well as for the future. It is about living as much as it is about dying. It is true that the gospel promises a kingdom in the future, a time when those who know Christ "will also reign with him" (2 Tim. 2:12). Like Christ's apostles, we too are waiting for the day to come when Jesus will "restore the kingdom to Israel" (Acts 1:6). But we do not have to wait to be placed under new authority. We do not yet see everything subject to Jesus, but we do see the one who has "tasted death" on our behalf (Heb. 2:9). Through Christ's death and resurrection, the Father "has rescued us from the dominion of darkness and brought us into the kingdom of the Son he loves" (Col. 1:13). As a result, the old dominion that sin once exercised over us has been shattered. Sin is our lord no longer (Rom. 6:14). The hope of the gospel is the hope of forgiveness, but it is also the expectation of "being strengthened with all power according to his glorious might" (Col. 1:11). Living the Christian life is more than a matter of willpower and information. The Christian life is Spirit driven and grace enabled. It is a life that is lived not only in response to the gospel but through the power of the gospel.

How Should We Preach?

How should this affect our preaching? Should we preach differently to believers than to unbelievers? The answer is both no and yes. In contemporary homiletics, the gospel sermon is usually treated as a separate genre of preaching with its own audience. Indeed, some churches base their entire ministry strategy on addressing the lost one way and those who are part of the church another. Yet Paul's epistles are proof enough that the saints need to hear the gospel even after they have believed. Paul's letters are also proof that the saints do not need to hear a different gospel after they have believed than the one that was preached to them prior to faith. The apostle was just as eager to preach the gospel to the saints at Rome as he was to proclaim it to those who had never heard Christ named (cf. Rom. 1:15 with 15:20).

While the saints do not need a different gospel, they do need a gospel which is explicated in terms of their experience. The difference between preaching the gospel to those who do not believe and to those who do is the difference between announcement and implication. Both involve obedience, but of a different sort. Martin Luther warned, "The chief article and foundation of the gospel is that before you take Christ as an example, you accept and recognize him as a gift, as a present that God has given you and that is your own."[20] When we announce the gospel to those who do not believe, we invite them to receive Christ as a gift. This is a call to the obedience of faith (Rom. 1:5). When we proclaim the gospel to the saints, we call them to take Christ as their example. But in doing so, we do not lose sight of the gift.

When we preach to saints, we focus on the "therefore" that proceeds from the gift. This too is the obedience of faith. It is the obedience which "comes from faith." When the gospel is preached to those who do not believe, it is faith itself which is the primary response which is called for. This faith is a response to God's gift and is itself a gift (Eph. 2:8–9). When we preach to those who have believed, we are calling for an obedience that springs from faith. We proclaim Christ as an example, but without losing sight of the fact that Christ and his righteousness have already been received as gifts. The gospel does not recede into the distance when preaching to the saints. It must remain in the forefront, or our call to take Christ as an example will prove toxic to those who hear. They will become like the Galatians, who after beginning with the Spirit, tried to attain their goal by human effort (Gal. 3:3).

Preaching which addresses the saints must differ from that which is addressed to unbelievers, because there is a fundamental difference between these two groups. To speak to the lost as if they are the same as the redeemed is a great mistake. Those who do not know Christ are fundamentally incapable of living the Christian life as it is described in the New Testament. They can be churchgoers. They can conform to some of the social and moral standards that are associated with cultural Christianity. But they cannot live the Christian life without receiving the life of Christ. Christian living depends upon the indwelling power of the Holy Spirit (Rom. 8:5–12).

To speak to the redeemed as if they were still lost is just as great a mistake. Certainly, there is value in reminding those who believe what they once were (Eph. 2:11–12; cf. Gal. 3:1–2; 1 Cor. 1:26). But our goal in preaching to the saints is to help them understand what is true of them now that they are in Christ. The chief aim of preaching the gospel to the redeemed is to remind them that they *are* the redeemed. They have been bought with a price and are not their own (1 Cor. 6:20). They are united with Christ in his death and resurrection and have the capacity to live a new life. As a result, they should no longer live as if they were still slaves to sin (Rom. 6:1–7).

Stanley Hauerwas observes, "Because contemporary Christian ethics have assumed that 'the ethical' primarily concerns action and decision, they have found little moral significance in basic affirmations about God, Christ, grace and sanctification."[21] Hauerwas counters that moral life for the Christian is actually a matter of attending to reality. Being a Christian, he notes, "involves more than just making certain decisions; it is a way of attending to the world. It is learning 'to see' the world under the mode of the divine."[22]

In making this observation, Hauerwas provides us with the primary rationale for preaching the gospel to the church. Yes, we are offering the hope of the gospel to any who may be among us who have not yet believed. But we are also providing those who believe with a view of the reality that will shape their response to our sermon. "A Christian does not simply 'believe' certain propositions about God; he learns to attend to reality through them," Hauerwas explains. "This learning requires training our attention by constantly juxtaposing our experience with our vision."[23]

Often both groups—the redeemed and those who are not yet believers—are part of the same audience. The same gospel applies to both. When we preach the gospel to those who are lost, we hold out the hope of Christ to them and call them to the obedience of faith. When we preach the gospel to those who already believe, we hold before them the Bible's vision of reality and call them to act accordingly.

Preaching Like Paul and Jesus

We should not mistake Paul's simple summary of his message for a lack of subtlety in its execution. He focused on "Jesus Christ and him crucified" (1 Cor. 2:2). Yet the biblical examples we have of Paul's preaching reveal someone who was keenly sensitive to his audience and to the context in which his message was delivered. He preached the same message to Jew and Gentile alike, but not necessarily in the same way. When preaching in the synagogue in Thessalonica, he reasoned from the Scriptures (Acts 17:2). In his approach to the philosophers on the Areopagus of Athens, he appealed to common experience, general revelation, and the observations of their own poets (Acts 17:16–34).

Nor should we conclude that the centrality of Christ in Paul's preaching means that Christ was the only thing Paul talked about in his preaching. Paul was a pastor as well as a missionary, and a theologian as well as a preacher. His letters suggest that he dealt with a full range of pastoral concerns in his preaching. Money, marriage, sex, and work all received his attention, not to mention the higher theological questions of creation, election and providence, and the lower concerns of church politics. Indeed, it seems likely that Paul's letters probably give us a more holistic sense of what his preaching must have been like than the few snippets of sermons that Luke preserves for us in the book of Acts.

Jesus' preaching too offers a model for our proclamation. William Brosend urges contemporary preachers to imitate Jesus' four main rhetorical strategies: to be dialogical, proclamatory, only occasionally self-referential, and persistently figurative. Dialogical preaching does not mean that we must turn the sermon into a lecture, giving listeners an opportunity to interrupt us and ask questions: "Dialogical preaching means asking yourself, often and repeatedly, in the beginning, middle and end of preparing your sermon: What questions do I imagine my listeners will bring with them? What questions will arise in the hearing of Scripture and sermon?"[24]

Proclamatory preaching is preaching that is not afraid to say what it must say. According to Brosend, it is declarative in nature: "It is decisive and clear, with our being willing to risk not always hearing 'Nice sermon, pastor' from listeners on the way out the door."[25] As for self-reference, Brosend argues that this technique is powerful only when it is not overused. In terms of its language, the preaching of Jesus teaches us to rely less on stock illustrations and learn to use the full range of figurative speech to convey our ideas. Vivid description, analogy, parable, hyperbole, story, even sarcasm and invective were just some of the tools Jesus used to craft his message. What is more, these were not wielded at random. Jesus' choice of language was shaped both by his purpose and an awareness of his audience.

We are not the first to preach. We stand in a long line of others who have gone before. All, save one, have been flawed like us. We can learn much from the methods they employed. But methodology, no matter how proven, is no substitute for the right message. This, in the end, is the root of our confidence every time we take our stand before the congregation. We are not ashamed of the gospel. It is the power of God.

chapter 9

PREACHING AS ORAL THEOLOGY

Preaching and theology were lovers once. Though inseparable and mutually devoted at the beginning of their relationship, they are now estranged. Not exactly enemies, they are hardly friends anymore, and they are certainly no longer partners. As is often the case in these matters, each blames the other for the separation. And as is also often the case, there is some truth in the complaint that each makes. Both are guilty of neglect.

Preaching and theology have since found more interesting companions, but this was not their original intent. They began their relationship with a common sense of purpose, supported by vows of mutual fidelity. To better accomplish their goal, they divided the work between them. Theology focused its attention on the higher matters of God, creation, and redemption, while preaching devoted itself to the lower but equally important concerns of the flock. They did not at first see these tasks as being mutually exclusive. Indeed, they believed that they contributed to one another.

Yet in time, the two grew apart. The noble questions which first occupied the attention of theology gave way to more obscure questions, at odds with the bread-and-butter interests of preaching. Theology preferred the thin air, heady conversation, and exclusive company of the classroom or the philosopher's salon to the dishrag speech and knee-scrape anxieties which occupied the attention of preaching. Preaching, for its part, grew impatient with the endless speculation and impractical theorizing that theology loved so much. Preaching criticized theology for being too detached. Theology accused preaching of being too parochial. The sad truth is that neither complaint was very far off the mark.

What Is the Matter with Theology?

What accounts for the divorce between theology and the pulpit in our day? Walter Wink's criticism, originally leveled against the state of New Testament studies in the mid-1970s, seems equally applicable to current evangelical theological scholarship. Wink described the American scholarly scene as "one of frenetic decadence, with the publication of vast numbers of articles and books which fewer and fewer people read."[1] The problem, according to Wink, was a toxic mixture of irrelevance combined with elitism: "Most scholars no longer address the lived experience of actual people in the churches or society. Instead they address the current questions of their peers in the professional scholarly guild."[2]

The divide between theology and preaching is partly attributable to this same tendency. The church does not value theology, because theologians are too busy conversing among themselves. Those who doubt this need only scan the list of topics to be addressed by speakers at any professional gathering of theologians and ask what bearing their subjects have on the "lived experience of actual people in the churches or society." The church is not interested in what theologians have to say because the questions that theologians address are not the questions that the church is asking.

It is true, of course, that we are not always the best judges of what we need to know. The mother who comes to church nearly beside herself with grief over her son's drug addiction is likely to find that her interest is not piqued by talk of the hypostatic union — the doctrine of Christ's two natures united in one person. She wants the preacher to give her something more concrete to help her get through her trial. She does not want theology. She wants Christ. Yet she brings her problems to Christ because she believes that Christ in his human nature can sympathize with her need, and she is confident that Christ in his divine nature can do something about it. She hopes to relate to Christ on a personal level, not as some theological abstraction scrawled in the margin of a scholar's manuscript. She looks to Christ because he is the Redeemer who has taken upon himself the sins of the world. Whether she recognizes it or not, all the comforts she hopes to get from the sermon are grounded in theology.

Still, we must admit that the church's suspicion of theology is not without some basis in experience. Helmut Thielicke's humorous portrait of the young theological student who comes home from seminary and unleashes his learning on an unsuspecting church reflects not only the perception of many laypeople when it comes to theology but their experience: "Under a considerable display of the apparatus of exegetical science and surrounded by the air of the initiated, he produces paralyzing and unhappy trivialities, and the inner muscular strength of a lively young Christian is horribly squeezed to death in a formal armor of abstract ideas."[3]

There is a speculative dimension to theology. In its healthy form, theological speculation enables us to uncover hidden depths of God's revealed truth. Theologians help us to probe questions we have not thought to ask on our own. But theology can also take unhealthy forms. It may elevate small points and magnify textual obscurities so that all the theologian offers the church are "paralyzing and unhappy trivialities." Congregational preaching offers a healthier climate for theological work than the academy. "When we preach from the Scriptures, to the congregation, the Bible is living in its native habitat," William Willimon suggests. "When the Bible is given over to scholars in some college department of religion who are subservient to the academy rather than the church, it is often made to answer questions that are of little interest to the originating intentions of Scripture itself."[4]

It is the tendency of theologians to focus on "the current questions of their peers in the professional scholarly guild" rather than the concerns of the pew that places the fruit of theological reflection out of reach for most believers. The use of academic language when discussing theology is only one of the factors which contribute to this. The problem is the theologian's aim. The goal of most theological writing today is not to theologize the church. The real prize is the recognition and respect of those in the guild. The best way to obtain these is by doing battle. Consequently, the theologian approaches his subject like a knight arrayed for combat, not like a shepherd concerned for the well-being of the flock. Theological discussion is a jousting match with other members of the guild.

Furthermore, theology's preoccupation with the interests of the guild breeds an air of condescension, if not outright contempt, toward those who are not members. The average church member senses this and concludes that the task of theological reflection is beyond his grasp. In this way, the guild mentality may actually foster the very theological ignorance it condemns. Since the guild is made up primarily of academics, the perspective of the majority of pastors is excluded from the conversation. As a result, many pastors read theology for their own amusement, but not for the sermon.

Preaching and Theology

Preaching must accept an equal share of the blame. Whether it is out of a sense of intellectual inadequacy or because of its own pragmatic bias, preaching has left theology in the hands of academics. Indeed, it may not be a case where academia has marginalized preaching and excluded the church from the theological conversation so much as it is one where preaching has marginalized theology and excluded it from the church. It is not the difficulty of theological constructs which has prompted this omission so much as it is the challenge of the pew. The preacher is not convinced that the theologian's structures can bear the full weight of the congregation's problems. Psychology and sociology seem to offer more concrete help, clothed as they are in the white-coated self-assurance of the scientific disciplines. Failing that, there is always the familiar comfort of common sense or the enthusiastic maxims of the motivational speaker, which are easily garnished with a Bible verse or two and made palatable for the church.

Preaching has lost confidence in theology, and preachers have forsaken their calling as the church's primary theologians. This is not surprising, considering the educational experience of most pastors. In the majority of seminaries and Bible colleges, pastoral theology is rarely treated as if it were "real" theology. Homiletics is taught as if it were just another speech class. Pastors are trained by theologians but are rarely taught to see themselves as theologians. They learn by experience to regard the concrete reality of Scripture, not the smoky abstractions of theology, as their primary field of interest.

Consequently, many preachers who are at home in the Bible are ill at ease when they cross the threshold of theology. Like visitors to some great and ancient mansion, they gaze awkwardly about, feeling that they are trespassing on someone else's domain. They move about its precincts like tourists, occasionally admiring the artifacts but hardly daring to handle them. How different it feels when they are tramping along the well-worn paths of Scripture. There they are in the company of old friends and familiar places. No wonder the preacher is so eager to forsake the marble-cold elegance of theology for the rough-hewn fellowship of those who inhabit the pages of the Bible.

Preaching is theological by nature because the Christian faith is doctrinal by nature. Doctrine cannot be removed from preaching without cutting the heart out of Christianity itself. " 'Christ died' — that is history; 'Christ died for our sins' — that is doctrine," J. Gresham Machen explains. "Without these two elements, joined in an absolutely indissoluble union, there is no Christianity."[5] Consequently, doctrine is at the root of all we believe in the Christian faith. Machen warns, "It must be admitted, then, that if we are to have a nondoctrinal religion, or a doctrinal religion founded merely on general truth, we must give up not only Paul, not only the primitive Jerusalem Church, but also Jesus Himself."[6] If we forsake doctrine, we abandon the basis for our hope and any ground we may have for application in the sermon.

Doctrine and Scripture are closely related but are not identical with one another. Paul implies a distinction between them in 2 Timothy 3:16 when he identifies doctrine or "teaching" as one of the things for which Scripture is "useful." What is the difference between the two? Scripture is the written record of what God has said. Doctrine is what the church teaches based upon what God has said. Scripture is a divine product. Doctrine is a result of human reflection. Doctrine shares the authority of Scripture only to the degree that it agrees with it. Defined this way, preaching and doctrine are synonymous. Preaching that is not doctrinal is not really preaching. Preaching is oral theology.

The Characteristics of Oral Theology

Oral theology is marked by three primary characteristics. It is local, narrative, and experiential. These characteristics are all related. The oral nature of preaching gives it a local character. Preaching addresses a specific audience in a particular setting. Lenora Tubbs Tisdale has described preaching as the practice of "local theology." For Tisdale, this is "theology that not only takes seriously larger church traditions, but that also attends with equal seriousness to the worldview, life experiences, and prior traditions" of the congregation.[7] The practice of local theology is reflected in contextualized preaching which shapes the sermon for a particular congregation that faces particular problems. It is preaching which not only recognizes the pastor's role as resident theologian but acknowledges the congregation's responsibility to think theologically.

Obviously, no theology can be entirely local and remain Christian. The practice of local theology does not mean that one congregation may affirm the deity of Christ or the value of his atoning death, while another has the liberty to reject those doctrines. Scripture's use of the definite article when speaking of "the faith" implies a fixed body of doctrines to which all believers must give their assent (1 Tim. 3:9; 4:1, 6; 6:21).

Yet even the Bible's articulation of its doctrines gives evidence of the local fires out of which its universal theological assertions were forged. The theological themes we identify with the books of the Bible reflect the particular circumstances which occasioned their writing. For Jonah, it was a parochial view of the interests and grace of "the God of heaven, who made the sea and the land" (Jonah 1:9). In Corinth, it involved, among other things, views of the ministry of the Holy Spirit and the relationship between the physical and the spiritual. These were overly influenced by Greek religion and philosophy. It is important to note that in both of these cases, biblical theology was actually in conflict with "local" assumptions about God. Local theology, then, is not the same thing as theological relativism. It is a result of applying the truth of God's Word to the questions and crises which arise within the congregation. Paul's letter to Philemon is a good example of this.

One of the most surprising features of the revealed theology of the Bible is its lack of systemization. "The faith" to which all believers must give assent is recorded in Scripture. But it is scattered throughout the pages of the Bible in a way which, if it were not for our conviction that God was behind it, might tempt us to describe it as haphazard. One of the most important contributions of systematic theology is its work of collating the data gathered from biblical exegesis and synthesizing it into a coherent theological construct for the church.

However, despite this benefit, systemization can also create problems. In some cases, the theologian's system may function like a child's Play-Doh factory. Here the system squeezes and twists the biblical text. Any data from the text which does not fit the system's presuppositions is pared away like clay which does not fit the Play-Doh mold. Theological systems can also reflect a cultural bias. This bias may be a function of demographics or a consequence of history. Writing about theological discourse on the global scene, Timothy C. Tennent observes, "Every culture in every age has blind spots and biases that we are often oblivious to, but which are evident to those outside of our culture or time. Every culture also has questions we all share in as members of Adam's race. Every culture also has questions and challenges peculiar to their particular context."[8]

Certainly, preaching can be systematic. There is nothing inherent in the oral nature of preaching that prohibits an orderly arrangement of ideas in sequence. But the oral quality of preaching provides a living dynamic which enables the preacher to address the questions and challenges which are peculiar to a congregation's own context. As unexpected circumstances arise or problems develop, the preacher leads the congregation in the collective practice of theological reflection. Those who hear respond by posing new questions which the preacher must now answer. A theological conversation is begun and the church collectively engages in the practice of biblical theology.

Narrative and Experiential

This living dynamic is a feature which oral theology shares in common with the Scriptures. The occasional nature of books of the Bible is not due to a lack of planning on God's part. Neither is it a result of the church's haphazard selection and arrangement of its religious texts. The reason the Bible's record of the theological experience of God's people is not linear is because life is not linear. This gives the theological content of the Bible a narrative and experiential quality which is at odds with most of the theological writing with which we are familiar.

Narrative is the Bible's predominant genre. Given the preference of Western culture for theology which is linear in its arrangement and is stated in propositional form, we might ask why this is so. Is it simply because "God loves stories"? Is story the spoonful of sugar which God provides to make the theological medicine go down? This may be partly true. But the ultimate reason is because biblical doctrine, contrary to contemporary theological practice, did not originate in the classroom. It arose out of the experience of God's people. Biblical narratives do more than tell stories. "They reveal God," Jeffrey Arthurs observes. "Sometimes Yahweh is the main 'character' of the story, as in the creation account (Genesis 1–2); sometimes he enters and exits the scene, as in the story of the tower of Babel (Genesis 12); and sometimes he is absent, as in the book of Esther. But even when seemingly absent, he silently permeates every scene, moving events, judging deeds, and motivating the players through love or dread."[9]

The characters who inhabit these stories enable us to interpret our own lives. Like Jacob, we too are on pilgrimage and wrestling with God. Like Esther, we must act in a world where the consequences of our decisions may be disastrous for us and where God's presence is not always evident. Like Simon Peter, the story of our attempt to follow Jesus seems to be marked by more failures than successes.

The prevalence of story in the Bible is a reflection of the church's pilgrimage of faith. This may explain why theology as it is currently taught holds so little appeal to the church today. Theology seems dead because it has been excised from the living context in which it originated. Like a body which has been exhumed from the grave, it retains its outward form but lacks a pulse. It has the shape of the living but the ghostly pallor of the dead.

Story is not the only framework the Bible uses to convey its doctrine. The Bible is also full of propositions. It contains poetry, prophecy, and law. In addition, there are a number of theological statements in the Scriptures which sound very much like formulas or creeds which were confessed by the congregation (1 Tim. 1:17; 3:16; 6:15–16). Yet the situation of God's people lies behind all of the Bible's propositions.

Paul's letters, for example, convey their doctrine in the form of proposition and are mostly linear in their arrangement. Yet by giving careful attention to the problems addressed, as well as to the apostle's tone and the offhand remarks he makes, a careful reader can often discern bits and pieces of the backstory which frames his assertions. Not enough, perhaps, to reconstruct it with complete certainty, but enough to discern the heartbeat.

Narrative is not always the best way to teach theology. It is doubtful that theological truth can be communicated without stating it in propositional form at some point in the sermon. Not everyone has the same learning style. Some respond to stories, while others need a more didactic approach. Preachers, too, vary in their ability to preach narrative sermons. A dull but clear proposition is often better than an interesting but vague narrative.[10]

David Wells reminds us that theology is not meant to be an end in itself. Theology's proper role is not as the object of our contemplation but as a servant to our spiritual life. "The Son of God assumed the form of a servant to seek and save the lost and theology must do likewise, incarnating itself in the cultural forms of its time without ever losing its identity as Christian theology," Wells explains. "God, after all, did not assume the guise of a remote Rabbi who simply declared the principles of eternal truth, but in the Son he compassionately entered into the life of ordinary people and declared to them what God's Word meant to them."[11]

The Bible's theology, then, is meant to be an incarnate theology. God's Word offers a view of life in which ordinary events are invested with theological significance. By paying attention to its stories and propositions, we not only learn from the experience of the men and women of faith who have gone before us; we discover that our lives too are invested with theological significance. In the act of preaching, the lived theology of the biblical text becomes the experienced theology of the congregation. This is not a function of a particular method of delivery. Rather it is the work of God's Spirit, who animates the story of our lives with the preached truth of the text.

THE END
OF PREACHING

During the last days of the Third Reich, as Allied bombs rained down on Stuttgart and the Nazi terror writhed in its final death throes, Helmut Thielicke preached a remarkable series of sermons based on the Lord's Prayer. These were days of uncertainty and death. On more than one occasion, the shriek of air raid sirens interrupted his sermon. Thielicke writes that during this period there were times when he felt utterly stricken: "My work in Stuttgart seemed to have gone to pieces; and my listeners were scattered to the four winds; the churches lay in rubble and ashes."[1]

In one of his messages, based upon the petition "Thy kingdom come," Thielicke describes an encounter with a woman from his congregation. He was standing in the street looking down into the pit of a cellar—all that remained from a building that an Allied bomb had shattered. The woman approached him and declared, "My husband died down there. His place was right under the hole. The clean-up squad was unable to find a trace of him; all that was left was his cap."

What does a pastor say in a moment like this? "I'm sorry" hardly seems adequate. But the woman had not come to Thielicke for sympathy. She wanted to express her gratitude. "We were there the last time you preached in the cathedral church," she continued. "And here before this pit I want to thank you for preparing him for eternity."[2]

This is as good a definition of preaching as I have heard. Better than many, perhaps, because of its stark realism. Preaching is preparing others for eternity. Preaching is having the last word. To preach is to take your stand before the pit and bear witness to the rubble of this ash-heap world that the kingdom of God is at hand. This woman's description of the aim of preaching is a sharp reminder that preaching is an eschatological act.

Preaching among the Ruins

What does it mean to describe preaching as eschatological? To many, the mention of eschatology brings to mind tent revivals, campground prophecy conferences, and warnings of imminent doom trumpeted from innumerable websites that scan the news for signs of Armageddon. Preaching is eschatological because it calls its hearers to live with the end in view. Preaching calls its hearers, as Jeremy Taylor writes, to dig their own graves and keep their own coffins in view.[3] Preaching reminds us that we are pilgrims who traverse an "empire of ruins" with death as our fellow traveler. Undeterred by our cold greeting and oblivious to the revulsion we feel at its presence, death pursues us tirelessly: "Death has climbed in through our windows and has entered our fortresses; it has cut off the children from the streets and the young men from the public squares" (Jer. 9:21).

Since we are unable to rid ourselves of this cheerless companion, we attempt to rehabilitate it instead, treating death as if it were a neighbor and not a trespasser. We clothe it in our best dress and apply makeup to its waxen features. Laid out before us in stiff repose, death looks as if it were merely asleep. If we do not examine it too carefully, we can almost persuade ourselves that it has a beating heart within its breast and warm blood pulsing through its veins. We whisper to ourselves that it is not as alien as we first thought. But this fool's dream vanishes the minute we attempt to embrace death, finding that it repays our kiss only with sorrow and loss.

We often speak of death as if it were a natural stage in the cycle of human development. But death is a curse (Gen. 2:17; Rom. 5:12). The presence of death is an intrusion. It is "natural" only to the extent that nature itself suffers from the stroke that fell upon Adam as a consequence of his sin. Nature endures death, but not willingly. It groans in protest, loathing the bondage to decay which death has brought upon it and yearning for "the glorious freedom of the children of God" (Rom. 8:21). Death is "the last enemy," a tyrant who acts on sin's behalf and whose sway over us, though finally broken at the cross, will be fully removed only at the resurrection (Rom. 5:21; 1 Cor. 15:26).

Helmut Thielicke illustrates death's alien nature in his account of a young flier who reached out to pick a bouquet of lilacs and uncovered the half-decayed body of a soldier beneath the bush: "He drew back in horror, not because he had never seen a dead man before—he drew back because of the screaming contradiction between the dead man and the flowering bush."[4] Thielicke notes that the flier's reaction would have been different if the man had come upon a dead and faded lilac bush instead: "A blooming lilac bush will one day become a withered lilac bush—this is really nothing more than the operation of the rhythm of life—but that a man should be lying there in a decayed condition, this was something that simply did not fit, and that's why he winced at the sight of it."[5]

We can understand the mystery of death only if we see it through the lens of Adam's rebellion against God. "That's why the barrier of death has been raised against us," Thielicke explains. "It teaches us that we men belong on this side of the border of transiency, that we are dust, that we are under judgment."[6] Death is the angel's flaming sword, an ever present reminder that the gates of Eden are now closed to us. However, if death is our enemy, it is also, like the law, a schoolmaster that leads us to Christ. Death's hard lesson exposes the true nature of sin (Rom. 7:13). Indeed, the law and death are allies in this mysterious work. Together they serve as God's goad, puncturing our denial and prodding us to turn to Christ for relief from death's sting (1 Cor. 15:56).

In Western culture, however, we have insulated ourselves from the evidence of death's presence. The medical necessities that accompany the end of life often result in a near quarantine of the dying that forces us to observe their passage from this life to the next from a distance. Most of the responsibilities involved in dispatching those who have succumbed to death are handled by paid professionals rather than by the church. The body is removed from sight as quickly as possible and prepared for burial by the hands of strangers. Burial is still officiated by the church but is organized by and often held at the funeral home. Hospitals and funeral homes provide necessary services. But the professionalization of this kind of care limits the role of the church and especially of the pastor. Instead of being a presence from last breath to final benediction, the church waits in the wings like a performer in the green room waiting to be called to the stage. When the invitation comes, the church enters the scene, offers a few words of comfort, provides a meal for the mourners, and then departs.

The tenor of the funeral has changed as well. Among the alterations that Thomas G. Long observes are a more festive tone, accompanied by a decreased emphasis on the formality of the service and on the presence of the dead body. Long notes the importance of this: "Our funerals are indeed changing, and that means something about how we view death is changing as well."[7] He warns that these changes have implications for the living as well as the dead: "To put it bluntly, a society that has forgotten how to honor the bodies of those who have departed is more inclined to neglect, even torture, the bodies of those still living. A society that has no firm hope for where the dead are going is also unsure how to take the hands of its children and lead them toward a hopeful future."[8]

Long's observations reminded me of the funeral I performed for a neighbor's son who had committed suicide. He was a hard-living man who plied the waters of the Illinois River working on a barge. During his life, he expressed little interest in God. God alone knows his heart, but by all outward appearances, this lack of interest did not change on the day he took his life. Like so many others in this sin-torn world, he lived without God and died without him.

I felt nervous when his parents asked me to perform the service. They were not churchgoing people. They did not want church music. Instead, they asked the funeral home to play "Proud Mary," the song made famous by Creedence Clearwater Revival. I breathed a sigh of relief when the funeral director politely informed the family that he didn't have a copy of that particular song on hand. But I worried that they might ask me to read the lyrics instead. I imagined myself standing before the coffin, reciting their preferred liturgy:

> *Big wheel keep on turnin',*
> *Proud Mary keep on burnin',*
> *Rollin', rollin', rollin' on the river.*

Thankfully, they did not ask me to do this. Instead, I preached a sermon about the foolish man who built his house on the sand: "The rain came down, the streams rose, and the winds blew and beat against that house, and it fell with a great crash" (Matt. 7:27).

But how do you offer comfort to people who have no reason to hope for comfort? What can you say to those whose loved ones have ordered their lives in such a way that they have left little room for God? I thought back to the advice we had been given in seminary for dealing with situations like this. The old-school preacher with a booming voice and a soft heart who taught us courses in preaching and pastoral care had urged, "Gentlemen, don't say anything about the destiny of their loved ones. Leave that to God. Just preach the hope of the gospel and make the condition of faith plain."

I confess that at the time I wondered if his approach wasn't a little soft. "After all, if these people have rejected Christ, why not come right out and say it?" I reasoned. "The shock might do the mourners some good." That was when I was young and brash. It was before pastoral ministry took me to the bedsides, emergency rooms, and funeral visitations of my congregation, where I learned to look into the hollow eyes of grief with more compassion.

Fortunately, being young and uncertain of myself, when the time came to do the funeral, I decided to follow my old professor's advice anyway. I chose to trade in hope, not despair. I preached the hope of the gospel, making the need for faith in Christ clear, and left judgment of the deceased in the hands of God.

But the modern fashion of focusing on life rather than death at funerals is symptomatic of a long-standing tendency to soften our language or avoid the subject altogether when it comes to death. We speak of death in euphemisms. We say that the dead have "passed on," "passed away," or "gone to a better place." We are equally loath to acknowledge that the dying will soon be dead, an unwillingness that results in an awkward silence when we are in the presence of the dying. In his book *How We Die*, Sherwin B. Nuland describes a personal instance of this involving a beloved aunt. Although she was dying of cancer, the family never discussed it with her. "She worried about us and we worried about her, each side certain it would be too much for the other to bear," Nuland writes. "We knew the outlook and so did she; we convinced ourselves she didn't know, though we sensed that she did, as she must have convinced herself we didn't know, though she must have known we did."[9]

A medical doctor, Nuland notes how this conspiracy of silence often leads to a futile pursuit of treatments which have little chance of success. "Pursuing treatment against great odds may seem like a heroic act to some, but too commonly it is a form of unwilling disservice to patients; it blurs the borders of candor and reveals a fundamental schism between the best interests of patients and their families on the one hand and of physicians on the other."[10] But the greatest tragedy of this conspiracy of silence is that it robs the living and the dying equally of the opportunity to prepare for this inevitable passage. Jeremy Taylor advised, "He that would die well must always look for death every day knocking at the gates of the grave; and then the gates of the grave shall never prevail upon him to do him mischief."[11]

The End of All Things

But it is not just our own end that draws near. It is "the end of all things" (1 Peter 4:7). Our listeners are passing away, as is this present world itself (1 Cor. 7:31; 1 John 2:17). Preaching that keeps the end in view reminds its hearers that we live in a dying world. Jesus spoke of the end of the age and the signs of his coming as something the church should anticipate eagerly (Matt. 24:3; cf. 13:36–43). After describing the signs that will mark the end, Jesus told his disciples, "When these things begin to take place, stand up and lift up your heads, because your redemption is drawing near" (Luke 21:28). Today we are as reluctant to speak to the congregation about the end of the age as we are to speak to the dying about their impending death. Eschatology has been caricaturized to the point where many who preach are embarrassed to mention the subject.

Our hesitancy to preach about the end times is not without explanation. It is partly because of differences over the hermeneutics of prophecy. We might feel less awkward about these differences if those who disagreed with us were our enemies. But they are our friends, fellow believers with whom we agree on the most important aspects of the Christian faith. So for the sake of Christian fellowship, we set our differences aside and agree to disagree. In many cases, this means we are silent on the subject, a practice which leads to a kind of functional relativism when it comes to eschatology. This is the sort of thing one hears when you ask someone about their view of Christ's return and they reply with a good-natured chuckle that they are panmillennial. "I believe it will all pan out in the end," they say with a smile.

If this is an admission that eschatological interpretation is difficult and beyond that person's understanding, then I have no quarrel. But if it is meant to imply that one view is as valid as another, we have a problem. The various views of the Lord's return are mutually exclusive. They can't all be right. Nor can they all be equally valid, not without being meaningless. There are important reasons for the differences between the views of Christ's return, for the most part because of disagreements over hermeneutical method. To act as if one view is as good as another is demeaning both to prophecy and to hermeneutics. I am not lobbying for a return to an era of open hostilities and bloodshed. But I do believe that frank disagreement which isn't afraid to label an opposing view as wrong is healthier than the kind of "don't ask, don't tell" relativism that marks our handling of the topic today.

Another reason we are largely silent on this topic is because our listeners would rather learn about the present earthly implications of the gospel than be told to wait for Jesus to appear. They have little use for a gospel which reserves the bulk of our hope for the future. They are too aware of the world's problems, too used to activism, and too inclined to take matters into their own hands to be satisfied with such a message. Their desire is essentially the same as that of the disciples in Acts 1:6: "Lord, are you at this time going to restore the kingdom to Israel?" They want more than a personal change. They want widespread systemic change. And they want it now.

But Jesus' answer to the disciples does not ease this tension. He does not say, "You guys have it all wrong. The kingdom has already arrived. You just need to recognize its present reality and integrate it into your social structures and relationships." Indeed, his answer sounds very much as if the kingdom was still in the future (Acts 1:7 – 8). This expectation is consistent with Jesus' model prayer, which taught his disciples to pray for the kingdom in a way that implies it is yet to come. The church has followed this pattern ever since, looking for the kingdom in the future, not in the present. Paul too, in his exhortation to the new converts in Lystra, Iconium, and

Antioch in Acts 14:21 – 22, held out the hope of a kingdom that was yet to come.

The End of Preaching

While waiting may not be to our taste, it is fundamental to the church's vocation, and has been from its inception. Immediately after the resurrection, the disciples were commanded by Jesus not to leave Jerusalem but to "wait for the gift my Father promised, which you have heard me speak about" (Acts 1:4). Yet even the coming of the Spirit did not put an end to waiting. Those who have received the firstfruits of the Spirit continue to "wait eagerly" for their adoption as sons (Rom. 8:23). This discipline of waiting is intrinsic to our hope. Hope that is seen is no hope at all. We hope for what we do not have and consequently "wait for it patiently" (Rom. 8:25). This kind of waiting is not passive. Eschatological waiting is marked by activism. Like the Thessalonians, we "serve the living and true God" and we "wait for his Son from heaven" (1 Thess. 1:9 – 10). It is a waiting marked by self-controlled, upright, and godly living by those who are eager to do good (Titus 2:12 – 14).

Preaching is an eschatological act which announces that the world is passing away along with its desires (1 John 2:17). This means that our gospel is a message of new beginnings as much as it is a gospel of endings. It announces that the night is nearly over and the day is almost here (Rom. 13:12). Just as the first rays of light appear before the sun rises above the horizon, "the darkness is passing and the true light is already shining" (1 John 2:8). We preach as Richard Baxter preached, "as never sure to preach again, and as a dying man to dying men." But we live like the apostle Paul, "as those who have been brought from death to life" (Rom. 6:13).

Therefore the hope we proclaim is both a present and a future hope. It is the hope of Israel — the expectation that the kingdom is still to come and the expectation that Jesus will one day sit enthroned in Jerusalem. But it is also the hope of heaven already brought near by the appearance of God in the flesh. As we wait for Christ's kingdom to come at a time that "the Father has set by his own authority," we bear witness to the world that Christ has already come and will come again. We act as agents of his kingdom in a world that has already been intersected by heaven and carry ourselves as those who have been rescued from the dominion of darkness and brought into the kingdom of the Son (Col. 1:13).

As citizens of Christ's kingdom, we live in a reality different from those who have not embraced the gospel. We inhabit a realm where it is possible for the two realities of heaven and earth to intersect, "so that there is an area in which the content of one belongs to the content of the other."[12] This is a world where it is possible for us to be in two places at once. We can stand beside the broken shell of a building contemplating the ravages of war and at the same time be seated with Christ in heavenly places (Eph. 2:6). Because God has become flesh and vanquished sin by his death and resurrection, we can pick our way through the rubble and still pray, "Thy kingdom come, thy will be done."

As preachers of Christ's kingdom, we bear witness to its initial incursion in the advent of Jesus Christ. We call upon those who have been transferred into its dominion from the domain of darkness to wait for it to appear in its fullness with the return of Jesus Christ (1 Thess. 1:10; Titus 2:13; Jude 1:21).

This is how Helmut Thielicke explained the sufferings he and his congregation experienced in his preaching. He described them as the intersection of two complementary lines of divine activity. One is a descending line of decay, "a line that ends in the terrors of the world which is its own destruction" and which are the evidence of God's judgment.[13] "For God's judgment does not consist in his destroying offenders with a thunderbolt from heaven," Thielicke explains. "It consists rather in his leaving them to their own wretchedness and compelling them to pursue their chosen road to the end, and go through every phase of its terrible curse."[14]

But alongside this is another line, which marks the mysterious advent of God's kingdom. "In the same measure as men turn away from God and go reeling on in drunkenness of their own misery so God's dominion on earth mysteriously goes on growing on earth — even now."[15] This is not the evolutionary development of human culture or the gradual Christianization of the world but the mysterious manifestation of Christ's presence. Thielicke finds it necessary to turn to Luther's theology of the presence of Christ in the Lord's Supper for a vocabulary to explain what he means: "In, with, and under the world's anguish and distress, in, with, and under the hail of bombs and mass murders, God is building his kingdom."[16]

Yet even with this analogy at his disposal, Thielicke confesses that he is at a loss for words: "We cannot explain it; we can only interpret it and follow its main lines. The kingdom of God is where Jesus Christ is. But Jesus always lingers in the darkest places of the world."[17]

This too is as good a definition of preaching as any I have heard. When we preach, we announce the incursion of Christ's kingdom into the dark places of the world. We declare that Jesus Christ has come and is coming again. Preaching traces the mysterious intersection of God's judgment and grace in the cross and points to the growing light which marks the swift approach of dawn. With mere words as its primary weapon, preaching topples the kingdom of death and unseats the dominion of darkness. Yet unlike the word of the Lord, which lasts forever, preaching will one day end. The day is drawing near when the church will no longer need its prophets, pastors, and teachers (1 Cor. 13:10; Eph. 4:11 – 13). When that day comes, all that is imperfect will pass away, and preaching along with it. Even so, come, Lord Jesus.

Amen.

ACKNOWLEDGMENTS

I am especially grateful to Ryan Pazdur and Paul Engle at Zondervan for their interest in and support for this project. Their conviction about the value of its message made its publication possible. I owe thanks to Grace Olson and Andy Jones for reading the initial manuscript and offering their valuable editorial insight. I am especially happy to be working with Brian Phipps again. His poetic eye is reflected in his editorial work. I am honored by Bryan Chapell's willingness to write the foreword during an especially busy season. His book *Christ-Centered Preaching* was one of the first that challenged me to think about the theological implications of the task of preaching. I owe more than a debt of thanks to Mark Sweeney for being my agent. Unfortunately for Mark, he must wait for heaven to reap his true reward. I want to express my love and gratefulness to my wife, Jane, who reads all my work and encourages me in this calling. Most of all, I give thanks to God for the inestimable privilege of declaring his Word.

NOTES

Chapter : Preface

1. Richard Lischer, *A Theology of Preaching: The Dynamics of the Gospel* (Eugene, Ore.: Wipf and Stock, 2001), 1.
2. Ibid.
3. Stephen H. Webb, *The Divine Voice: Christian Proclamation and the Theology of Sound* (Grand Rapids, Mich.: Brazos, 2004), 36.

Chapter 1: Folly, Grace, and Power

1. O. C. Edwards Jr., *A History of Preaching*, vol. 2 (Nashville: Abingdon, 2004), 536.
2. Ibid., 539.
3. Eugene Peterson, *Eat This Book* (Grand Rapids, Mich.: Eerdmans, 2006), 31.
4. Ibid., 30.
5. Jean Kilbourne, "Jesus Is a Brand of Jeans," *New Internationalist*, September 2004, 10–12, emphasis in original.
6. Jeremy S. Begbie, "Beauty, Sentimentality, and the Arts," in *The Beauty of God: Theology and the Arts*, ed. Daniel J. Treier, Mark Husbands, and Roger Lundin (Downers Grove, Ill.: InterVarsity, 2007), 46–47.
7. Don Hudson, "The Glory of His Discontent: The Inconsolable Suffering of God," *Mars Hill Review*, June 1996: 21–33.
8. Helmut Thielicke, *Christ and the Meaning of Life: Sermons and Meditations* (London: Clarke, 1962), 44.
9. Karl Barth, *Homiletics* (Louisville: Westminster/John Knox, 1991), 47.
10. Ibid., 48.
11. John Calvin, *Institutes of the Christian Religion*, 4.8.2 (Louisville: Westminster/John Knox, 1960), 1151.
12. Stephen H. Webb, *The Divine Voice* (Grand Rapids, Mich.: Brazos, 2004), 14.
13. Ibid., 36.

14. Martyn Lloyd-Jones, *Preaching and Preachers* (Grand Rapids, Mich.: Zondervan, 1971), 58.

Chapter 2: The Untamed Spirit and the Sermon

1. Martyn Lloyd-Jones, *Preaching and Preachers* (Grand Rapids, Mich.: Zondervan, 1971), 298.
2. Charles G. Finney, *Lectures on Revivals of Religion* (New York: Leavitt, Lord, and Co. 1835), 12.
3. Ibid., 34.
4. Ibid., 43.
5. William Willimon, *The Intrusive Word: Preaching to the Unbaptized* (Grand Rapids, Mich.: Eerdmans, 1994), 20.
6. Ibid., 22.
7. Jeffrey A. Mullins, "'Fitted to Receive the Word of God': Emotions and Scientific Naturalism in the Religious Revivals of the 1830s," *International Social Science Review* 81, nos. 1–2 (2006): 4.
8. Ibid., 40.
9. Grant Osborne, *The Hermeneutical Spiral* (Downers Grove, Ill.: InterVarsity, 1991), 340.
10. Charles Spurgeon, *Second Series of Lectures to My Students* (New York: Robert Carter and Brothers, 1889), 22.
11. Ibid., 24.
12. John Calvin, *Institutes of the Christian Religion* 1.8.5 (Louisville: Westminster/John Knox, 1960), 80.
13. Jonathan Edwards, *A Treatise Concerning Religious Affections in Three Parts* (Philadelphia: James Crissy, 1821), 16–17.
14. It is possible, of course, that Luke records only a synopsis of what Peter said and not the entire sermon.
15. Lloyd-Jones, *Preachers and Preaching*, 118–19.
16. Abraham Kuyper, *The Work of the Holy Spirit*, trans. Henri De Vries (New York: Funk and Wagnals, 1900), 38.

Chapter 3: The Human Side of Preaching

1. Charles Spurgeon, *Second Series of Lectures to My Students* (New York: Robert Carter and Brothers, 1889), 30.
2. John Henry Jowett, *The Preacher, His Life and Work* (New York: Harper and Brothers, 1912), 45.
3. Ibid., 46.
4. John R. W. Stott, *Between Two Worlds: The Art of Preaching in the Twentieth Century* (Grand Rapids, Mich.: Eerdmans, 1982), 267.
5. J. I. Packer, *Evangelism and the Sovereignty of God* (Downers Grove, Ill.: InterVarsity, 1961), 23.
6. Karl Barth, *Homiletics* (Louisville: Westminster/John Knox, 1991), 44.
7. Ibid., 45.
8. Phillips Brooks, *Lectures on Preaching* (New York: Dutton, 1902), 8.

9. Ibid.
10. Eugene Peterson, *Eat This Book: A Conversation in the Art of Spiritual Reading* (Grand Rapids, Mich.: Eerdmans, 2006), 85.
11. Ibid., 86.
12. Stephen H. Webb, *The Divine Voice: Christian Proclamation and the Theology of Sound* (Grand Rapids, Mich.: Brazos, 2004), 208.
13. O. C. Edwards Jr., *A History of Preaching*, vol. 2 (Nashville: Abingdon, 2004), 538.
14. David Wells, "The Nature and Function of Theology," in *The Use of the Bible in Theology*, ed. Robert K. Johnston (Atlanta: John Knox, 1983), 176.
15. Ibid.
16. Scot McKnight, "The Jesus We'll Never Know," *Christianity Today*, April 2010, 23.
17. George MacDonald, "The New Name," in *Unspoken Sermons* (London: Alexander Strahan, 1867), 110–11.
18. Ibid., 111.

Chapter 4: Preaching and Authority

1. David Buttrick, *Homiletic: Moves and Structures* (Philadelphia: Fortress, 1987), 241.
2. Ibid., 243.
3. Thomas G. Long, *The Witness of Preaching* (Louisville: Westminster/John Knox, 2005), 23–24.
4. Buttrick, *Homiletics*, 240.
5. Ibid., 241.
6. Ibid., 243.
7. John Calvin, *Institutes of the Christian Religion*, 4.8.2 (Louisville: Westminster/John Knox, 1960), 1150.
8. Ibid., 4.
9. Sallie McFague Teselle, "Parable, Metaphor and Theology," *Journal of the American Academy of Religion* 42, no. 4 (December 1974): 643.
10. J. Gresham Machen, *Christianity and Liberalism* (Grand Rapids, Mich.: Eerdmans, 1923), 71.
11. Ibid., 72.
12. Long, *The Witness of Preaching*, 46.
13. J. H. Jowett, *The Preacher, His Life and Work* (New York: Hodder and Stoughton, 1912), 61.

Chapter 5: Speaking for the Silent God

1. Andy Crouch, *Culture Making: Recovering Our Creative Calling* (Downers Grove, Ill.: InterVarsity, 2008), 20.
2. John Calvin, *Institutes of the Christian Religion*, 1.5.1, ed. John T. McNeill, 2 vols. (Philadelphia: Westminster, 1960), 1:52.
3. Helmut Thielicke, "World History and World Judgment," in *Christ and the Meaning of Life: Sermons and Meditations*, trans. John W. Doberstein (London: Clarke, 1962), 13.

4. See also Rom. 1:20, where Paul speaks of God's "invisible qualities."

5. Thielicke, "World History and World Judgment," 13.

6. Moses was a prototype of the prophetic office, but he was not the first human representative to speak for God. Noah is called a "preacher of righteousness" in 2 Peter 2:5. The Scriptures, however, do not provide any examples of what Noah said.

7. Jeremy S. Begbie, *Resounding Truth: Christian Wisdom in the World of Music* (Grand Rapids, Mich.: Baker, 2007), 285.

8. David Buttrick, *Homiletic: Moves and Structures* (Philadelphia: Fortress, 1987), 239.

9. Ibid., 242.

10. Timothy Ward, *Words of Life: Scripture as the Living and Active Word of God* (Downers Grove, Ill.: InterVarsity, 2009), 31–32.

11. Benjamin Breckinridge Warfield, *The Inspiration and Authority of the Bible* (Phillipsburg, Penn.: Presbyterian and Reformed, 1948), 299.

12. Ibid. Warfield offers Gal. 3:8 (which cites Gen. 11:1–2) and Rom. 9:17 (which cites Exod. 9:16) as examples of the first. He offers Matt. 19:4–5 (which cites Gen. 2:24), Heb. 3:7 (which cites Ps. 95:7), Acts 4:24–25 (which cites Ps. 2:1), and many others as examples of the second.

13. John R. W. Stott, "Christian Preaching in the Contemporary World," *Bibliotheca Sacra* 145, no. 580 (October–December 1988): 365.

14. John R. W. Stott, *Between Two Worlds: The Challenge of Preaching Today* (Grand Rapids, Mich.: Eerdmans, 1982), 125–26.

Chapter 6: Word and Sermon

1. Fred Lybrand seems to make such an argument when he writes, "The hope for the manuscripter is that the Spirit of God was leading when the text was written because the Spirit has no room to lead during delivery. With a read sermon the Spirit can't say, 'Stop.' Instead, we tell him 'Use this!'" (Fred Lybrand, *Preaching on Your Feet: Connecting God and the Audience in the Preachable Moment* [Nashville: Broadman, 2008], 47).

2. J. I. Packer, "The Adequacy of Human Language," in *Inerrancy*, ed. Norman L. Geisler (Grand Rapids, Mich.: Zondervan, 1980), 211.

3. B. B. Warfield, *The Inspiration and Authority of Scripture* (Phillipsburg, Penn.: Presbyterian and Reformed, 1948), 93.

4. Ibid.

5. F. F. Bruce, *The Acts of the Apostles* (Grand Rapids, Mich.: Eerdmans, 1951), 26–27. Luke's style was shaped both by dramatic intent and by his sources. See J. De Zwann, "The Greek of Acts," in *The Acts of the Apostles*, vol. 2, *Criticism*, ed. F. J. Foakes Jackson and Kirsopp Lake (Grand Rapids, Mich.: Baker, 1979), 64.

6. Kerry Inman cites the extensive analysis by Edwin A. Abbot when he notes that John "handles the New Testament vocabulary in a distinctive way" (V. Kerry Inman, "Distinctive Johannine Vocabulary and the Interpretation of 1 John 3:9," *Westminster Theological Journal* 40, no. 1 [Fall 1997]: 136–44).

7. This analogy is derived from Dallas Willard's description of the physical body as the realm of human dominion: "In creating human beings in his likeness so that we could govern in his manner, God gave us a measure of *independent* power. Without such power, we absolutely could not resemble God in the close manner in which he intended, nor could we be God's co-workers. *The locus or depository of this necessary power is the human body.* This explains, in theological terms, why we have a body at all. *That body is our primary area of power, freedom, and—therefore—responsibility*" (Dallas Willard, *Spirit of the Disciplines: Understanding How God Changes Lives* [San Francisco: HarperSanFrancisco, 1988], 53, emphases in original).

8. Karl Barth, *Homiletics* (Louisville: Westminster/John Knox, 1991), 45.

9. Leon Morris, *The Atonement: Its Meaning and Significance* (Downers Grove, Ill.: InterVarsity, 1983), 152.

10. Thomas G. Long, *Preaching from Memory to Hope* (Louisville: Westminster/John Knox, 2009), 35.

11. Neil Postman, *Technopoly* (New York: Vintage, 1993), 124.

12. Charles Sherlock, *The Doctrine of Humanity* (Downers Grove, Ill.: InterVarsity, 1996), 144.

13. John McWhorter, *Doing Our Own Thing: The Degradation of Language and Music and Why We Should, Like, Care* (New York: Gotham, 2003), 35.

14. Ibid., 47.

15. Ibid., 69–70.

16. Ibid., 67.

17. Rosalie de Rosset, "Felling the Devil," in *The Moody Handbook of Preaching*, ed. John Koessler (Chicago: Moody, 2008), 248.

18. George Orwell, "Politics and the English Language," in *George Orwell: Essays* (New York: Knopf, 2002), 954.

19. Ibid., 963.

20. Augustine, *On Christian Doctrine*, book IV, 11.25, trans. D. W. Robertson Jr. (Indianapolis: Bobbs-Merrill, 1958), 136.

21. Ibid., book IV, 12.27.

22. C. S. Lewis, *An Experiment in Criticism* (Cambridge: Cambridge Univ. Press, 1961), 32–33.

23. Jonathan Edwards, "The Great Concern of a Watchman of Souls," quoted by Douglas A. Sweeney in *Jonathan Edwards and the Ministry of the Word* (Downers Grove, Ill.: InterVarsity, 2009), 136.

Chapter 7: Prophet, Priest, or Stand-Up Comedian?

1. Thomas G. Long, *The Witness of Preaching*, 2nd ed. (Louisville: Westminster/John Knox, 2005), 18.

2. Calvin Miller urges preachers to learn from the style of anchorpersons on the six o'clock news: "They read the text in so casual and direct a way that they appear to be utterly spontaneous in the unfailing roll of words that flow from their lips" (Calvin Miller, *Marketplace Preaching: How to Return the Sermon to Where It Belongs* [Grand Rapids, Mich.: Baker, 1995], 48). Others try to imitate

the goofy friendliness and class-clown nonchalance of late-night talk-show hosts. See Dennis Beatty and Elizabeth E. Beatty, "Comedy Club Pastor: How a Course in Stand-Up Invigorated My Preaching," *Leadership* 22, no. 2 (Spring 2001): 111–14.

3. Neil Postman, *Amusing Ourselves to Death* (New York: Penguin, 1985), 118.

4. James B. Twitchell, *Carnival Culture: The Trashing of Taste in America* (New York: Columbia Univ. Press, 1992), 200.

5. Geoffrey Wainwright, "Preaching as Worship," *Greek Orthodox Theological Review* 28, no. 4 (Winter 1983): 328. The sacrifice Paul has in view in these verses is not the sermon but the Gentiles who had become sanctified by the Holy Spirit through the gospel. In the apostle's analogy, preaching is not the offering but the knife used to prepare the offering.

6. Frederick Buechner, *Telling the Truth: The Gospel as Tragedy, Comedy and Fairy Tale* (New York: Harper, 1977), 35.

7. Thomas G. Long, *Preaching from Memory to Hope* (Louisville: Westminster/ John Knox, 2009), 38.

8. Annie Dillard, *Pilgrim at Tinker Creek* (New York: Harper, 1974), 236.

9. Ibid., 242.

10. Northrop Frye, *The Educated Imagination* (Bloomington: Indiana Univ. Press, 1964), 63–64.

11. Ibid., 64.

12. C. S. Lewis, *God in the Dock* (Grand Rapids, Mich.: Eerdmans, 1970), 66.

13. Rudolf Bultmann, "New Testament and Mythology," in *Kerygma and Myth: A Theological Debate*, ed. Hans Werner Barsch (New York: Harper, 1961), 1–16.

14. Lewis, *God in the Dock*, 66, emphases in original.

15. Ibid.

16. John Ker, *The Day Dawn and the Rain, and Other Sermons* (New York: Robert Carter and Brothers, 1869), 62.

17. Ibid, 60.

18. Ibid.

19. Ibid., 62.

Chapter 8: Preaching as Gospel

1. Joachim Jeremias, *New Testament Theology*, trans. John Bowden (New York: Charles Scribner's Sons, 1971), 29.

2. Ibid., 30.

3. I. Howard Marshall, *The Gospel of Luke*, The New International Greek Testament Commentary (Grand Rapids, Mich.: Eerdmans, 1978), 323.

4. Jeremias, *New Testament Theology*, 96.

5. William Brosend, *The Preaching of Jesus: Gospel Proclamation Then and Now* (Louisville: Westminster/John Knox, 2010), 18.

6. Ibid., 13.

7. Ibid., 23.

8. Ibid., 22.

9. Ibid., 13, 24.

10. Thomas Dehany Bernard, *The Progress of Doctrine in the New Testament* (Boston: Gould and Lincoln, 1869), 131.

11. Acts 8:12; 14:22; 19:8; 20:25; 28:23, 31; cf. Rom. 14:17; 1 Cor. 4:20; 6:9–10; 15:24, 50; Gal. 5:21; Eph. 5:5; Col. 1:12–13; 4:11; 1 Thess. 2:12; 2 Thess. 1:5; 2 Tim. 4:1, 8; Heb. 12:28; James 2:5; 2 Peter 1:11; Rev. 1:6, 9; 5:10; 11:15; 12:10.

12. Bernard, *The Progress of Doctrine in the New Testament*, 133; cf. Acts 28:23, 31.

13. Ibid., 135.

14. Rom. 10:8; 1 Cor. 1:18; 2 Cor. 5:19; Col. 4:3; Eph. 1:13; Col. 1:5; Rom. 1:1–2, 9, 15–17; 2:16; 11:28; 15:16, 19–20; 16:25; 1 Cor. 1:17; 9:14, 16, 18, 23; 15:1–2; 2 Cor. 2:12; 4:3–4; 10:14, 16; 11:7; Gal. 2:2, 7; 4:13; Eph. 3:7; 6:19; Phil. 1:7, 12, 16; 2:22; 4:3, 15; Col. 1:23; 1 Thess. 2:2, 4, 8–9; 3:2; 2 Thess. 2:14; 1 Tim. 1:11; 2 Tim. 1:8, 10–11; 2:8; Philem. 1:13.

15. Thomas F. Torrance, *Preaching Christ Today: The Gospel and Scientific Thinking* (Grand Rapids, Mich.: Eerdmans, 1994), 1.

16. Ibid., 9–10.

17. Ibid., 55.

18. Richard Lischer, *A Theology of Preaching: The Dynamics of the Gospel* (Eugene, Ore.: Wipf and Stock, 2001), 25.

19. Torrance, *Preaching Christ Today*, 30–31.

20. Martin Luther, "A Brief Instruction on What to Look for and Expect in the Gospels," in *Martin Luther's Basic Theological Writings*, ed. Timothy F. Lull (Minneapolis: Augsburg Fortress, 2005), 95.

21. Stanley Hauerwas, *Vision and Virtue* (Notre Dame: Univ. of Notre Dame Press, 1974), 45.

22. Ibid., 45–46.

23. Ibid., 46.

24. Brosend, *The Preaching of Jesus*, 29.

25. Ibid.

Chapter 9: Preaching as Oral Theology

1. Walter Wink, "How I Have Been Snagged by the Seat of My Pants While Reading the Bible," *Christian Century*, September 24, 1975, 816.

2. Ibid.

3. Helmut Thielicke, *A Little Exercise for Young Theologians*, trans. Charles L. Taylor (Grand Rapids, Mich.: Eerdmans, 1962), 8.

4. William Willimon, *Proclamation and Theology* (Nashville: Abingdon, 2005), 34.

5. J. Gresham Machen, *Christianity and Liberalism* (Grand Rapids, Mich.: Eerdmans, 1923), 27.

6. Ibid., 45.

7. Lenora Tubbs Tisdale, *Preaching as Local Theology and Folk Art* (Minneapolis: \ Fortress, 1997), 39.

8. Timothy C. Tennent, *Theology in the Context of World Christianity* (Grand Rapids, Mich.: Zondervan, 2007), 12.

9. Jeffrey D. Arthurs, "Preaching the Old Testament Narratives," in *Preaching the Old Testament*, ed. Scott M. Gibson (Grand Rapids, Mich.: Baker, 2006), 74.

10. John Koessler, "Why All the Best Preachers Are Theological," in *The Art and Craft of Biblical Preaching*, ed. Haddon Robinson and Craig Brian Larson (Grand Rapids, Mich.: Zondervan, 2005), 246.

11. David Wells, "The Nature and Function of Theology," in *The Use of the Bible in Theology: Evangelical Options*, ed. Robert K. Johnston (Louisville: John Knox, 1985), 195.

Chapter 10: The End of Preaching

1. Helmut Thielicke, *The Prayer That Spans the World: Sermons on the Lord's Prayer*, trans. James Doberstein (Cambridge: James Clarke, 1953), 65.

2. Ibid., 66.

3. Jeremy Taylor, *The Rule and Exercises of Holy Dying* (London: John Henry and James Parker, 1857), vi.

4. Helmut Thielicke, *Christ and the Meaning of Life* (Cambridge: James Clarke and Co., 1965), 35.

5. Ibid.

6. Ibid., 37.

7. Thomas G. Long, *Accompany Them with Singing: The Christian Funeral* (Louisville: Westminster/John Knox, 2009), 7.

8. Ibid.

9. Sherwin B. Nuland, *How We Die: Reflections on Life's Last Chapter* (New York: Knopf, 1994), 244.

10. Ibid., 246.

11. Taylor, *The Rule and Exercises of Life*, 45.

12. Thomas F. Torrance, *Preaching Christ Today: The Gospel and Scientific Thinking* (Grand Rapids, Mich.: Eerdmans, 1994), 52.

13. Thielicke, *The Prayer That Spans the World*, 59.

14. Ibid., 57.

15. Ibid., 59.

16. Ibid., 60.

17. Ibid.

A Stranger in the House of God

From Doubt to Faith and Everywhere in Between

John Koessler

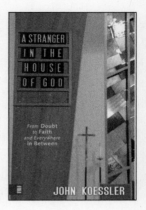

Growing up the son of agnostics, John Koessler saw a Catholic church on one end of the street and a Baptist on the other. In the no-man's land between the two, this curious outsider wondered about the God they worshiped — and began a lifelong search to comprehend the grace and mystery of God.

A Stranger in the House of God addresses fundamental questions and stuggles faced by spiritual seekers and mature believers. Like a contemporary Pilgrim's Progress, it traces the author's journey and explores his experiences with both charismatic and evangelical Christianity. It also describes his transformation from religious outsider to ordained pastor.

John Koesller provides a poignant and often humorous window into the interior of th soul as he describes his journey from doubt and struggle with the church to personal faith.

www.JohnKoessler.com

Share Your Thoughts

With the Author: Your comments will be forwarded to the author when you send them to *zauthor@zondervan.com*.

With Zondervan: Submit your review of this book by writing to *zreview@zondervan.com*.

Free Online Resources at
www.zondervan.com

Zondervan AuthorTracker: Be notified whenever your favorite authors publish new books, go on tour, or post an update about what's happening in their lives at www.zondervan.com/authortracker.

Daily Bible Verses and Devotions: Enrich your life with daily Bible verses or devotions that help you start every morning focused on God. Visit www.zondervan.com/newsletters.

Free Email Publications: Sign up for newsletters on Christian living, academic resources, church ministry, fiction, children's resources, and more. Visit www.zondervan.com/newsletters.

Zondervan Bible Search: Find and compare Bible passages in a variety of translations at www.zondervanbiblesearch.com.

Other Benefits: Register to receive online benefits like coupons and special offers, or to participate in research.

ZONDERVAN.com/
AUTHORTRACKER
follow your favorite authors